Tackle Athletics

By the same author

Athletics for Women
(with D. L. Pugh)

Schoolgirl Athletics

The Complete Middle Distance Runner
(with H. Wilson and F. Horwill)

Denis Watts

Tackle ATHLETICS

Stanley Paul · London

Stanley Paul & Co Ltd
3 Fitzroy Square, London W1

An imprint of the Hutchinson Publishing Group

London Melbourne Sydney Auckland
Wellington Johannesburg Cape Town
and agencies throughout the world

First published 1964
Second edition June 1968
This edition 1974
© Denis Watts 1964

Set in Monotype Imprint
Printed in Great Britain by The Anchor Press Ltd
and bound by Wm Brendon & Son Ltd
both of Tiptree, Essex

ISBN 0 09 122240 0 (cased)
      0 09 122241 9 (paper)

Contents

Illustrations

Introduction

This book is not just a reiteration of universally accepted techniques for the more popular events, but a positive attempt to put the young athlete on the right path to become a champion. Only the essential technical points are dealt with in detail, the main emphasis being the mental and physical preparation of the young athlete for success in major competition.

Correct technique in all events is the first essential of success; without it the thrower, jumper or hurdler can never hope to be successful in his chosen sphere. However, technique and strength go hand in hand, so often the young athlete is unable to perform his event correctly because he lacks the physical strength. No matter how many times the coach may say 'Do it this way', he fails because he is physically incapable of applying the necessary force or handling his bodyweight in the correct manner. This applies to the throwing and jumping events in the main, but also, to a lesser extent, to running and hurdling.

Mobility and range of movement are also essential to the good performance of athletic skills. Suppling and mobilizing work must be carried out alongside the weight training and/or isometric training. In this way the hurdler may obtain sufficient 'split' across the hurdle. The runner may apply his force over a greater distance by correct use of the hips and obtain a high knee lift of the recovery leg. The javelin thrower may pull directly along the shaft of his spear from a position where the arm is fully extended to the rear of his shoulder. The high jumper can utilize a high and straight swing of the non-jumping leg, thus gaining valuable momentum at take-off. These are just a few examples of the necessity for possessing the quality of mobility.

Finally, the athlete must develop the mental qualities of determination, resilience and singleness of purpose—determination to be first, resilience to the discouraging effects or failure and refusal to deviate from the narrow path towards the ultimate goal.

1. Sprinting

The vast improvement in the standard of sprinting in the country over the last decade has been brought about largely through improved methods of training. In the past it was considered sufficient to begin work in March, training perhaps three or four days per week.

Today our great sprinters train six to seven days a week, commencing after a short rest of about a month at the close of the season. A large part of this training is done at speed, including starting without the gun, and serious interval running on the track over varying distances. Many sprinters also use progressive resistance exercises as an adjunct to their weekly programme in order to develop power by training for muscular strength. Development of power is by far the most profitable line to pursue in order to increase speed over the shorter distances. Given sufficient natural ability, the rest is just a matter of dedication to hard work. Hard work in training builds a capacity for even harder work and general fitness and strength improve from week to week and month to month.

The sprinter also has to consider certain points of technique, such as the start and pick-up, bend running and a controlled finish. The start is all-important in the 100 m and 200 m where a poor getaway may well lose the race. Bend running is vital in the 200 m; the runner who is capable of negotiating the bend correctly can come out into the straight 2 or 3 m to the good over his less experienced rivals. Peter Radford is a classic example of a great bend runner and because of this took the first leg for the English 4 × 100 m relay team at Perth in 1962. By his superb technique on the curve, he laid the foundations of England's victory in the new Commonwealth and Empire Games record of 40·6 sec.

The Start

It is essential for the sprinter to adopt a position at the start which enables him to accelerate rapidly away from his blocks. Comfort is not necessarily the criterion of a satisfactory position; sometimes discomfort may be experienced expecially when using blocks for the first time. The sprinter must adapt himself to the best possible position and learn to handle it correctly over a period.

It is recommended that the blocks be set at the approximate angles of 45 degrees for the front block and 80 degrees for the rear block. The spacing between blocks should be about 16 in., plus or minus a little bit. The distance of the front block from the starting line will vary with the individual; it depends mainly on the physique and rate of acceleration. The average distance is generally found to fall within 15 in. and 20 in. It is best to obtain the advice of a competent coach when deciding what starting position to adopt. It is possible to settle on the best position only after a considerable amount of starting practice. Remember the start is not just leaving the blocks but accelerating over at least the first 40 m of the race.

'On Your Marks'

On the command 'On your marks' you should:

1. Walk forward from the marshalling line, back into your blocks, placing both feet firmly against them with the toes touching the ground.

2. Your hands should be situated behind the line with the fingers forming a high bridge, thumb and first finger up to the line.

3. Your shoulders should be inclined forward so that a plumb line dropped from them would fall about 2 in. in front of your hands and the starting line.

4. Your rear knee should rest on the ground approximately in line with your instep or big-toe joint of the front foot. Looking from the front there should be a gap of about 2 in. between the instep and the knee.

5. Keep your head in line with your back and focus your eyes about a yard in front of your hands.

The 'Set' Position

On the command 'Set' you should:

1. Raise your hips steadily into a position where they are in line or slightly higher than the shoulders. The exact position will vary with the individual; some sprinters require a much higher hip position than others.

2. Brace your fingers and keep your arms straight but not locked at the elbows. Your upper body must rise immediately the gun is fired; it is, therefore, advantageous to have some play at the elbows.

3. The angle at your front knee should be approximately 90 degrees and rear knee 110–120 degrees.

4. As you rise into the set position take a breath and hold it. This will fix the muscles of the thorax and gives the legs something firm to work against.

5. Concentrate your thoughts on the action of running; the gun is merely the stimulus which triggers-off your movement.

The Gun

When the gun is fired you should:

1. Keep your upper body parallel to the ground while your front foot is driving against the block.

2. After its initial drive your rear leg should be pulled through fast into the first stride.

3. Keep your trunk low and concentrate on high knee pick-up under a low body. Your trunk should not come upright until some eight to ten strides have been covered.

4. Concentrate now on a forceful thrust of the driving leg and range of movement between the thighs.

5. Incorporate a forceful balancing action of the arms—think of pulling your elbows back. An efficient arm action is of vital importance to you.

The 'Pick-Up'

1. After eight to ten strides your body should have reached its natural sprinting angle. This will mean that some body lean is still being held in the majority of cases.

2. You should now emphasize a high knee pick-up of your recovery leg; this will assist with momentum and drive.

3. Your arms should be moved forcefully from the shoulders, held at an angle of 90 degrees at the elbows. If anything they should be at more than 90 degrees rather than less.

4. Try to obtain a complete extension of the driving leg behind the hip.

5. Your head must maintain a relaxed position in natural alignment with the back. Pull your chin in and relax the neck and shoulders muscles.

The Finish

1. Maintain your powerful arm action to assist your legs.
2. Don't chop your stride in an attempt to gain leg speed. Maintain the range of movement of your leg action.
3. Keep your head in line with your back and hold a slight forward lean of the trunk.
4. A chest drop or shoulder turn may be employed when you are more experienced. However, the ability to do this depends largely upon where your foot lands in relation to the finishing line.

200 m

The novice should think of the race as having three parts — the start and pick-up to full speed covering the first 60 m, the coast in the middle part of the race and the finish. His aim, as he progresses and improves, should be to run the whole race as one unit with only a slight drop in tension in the middle part of the race.

The Start

The start is on the bend and, therefore, the blocks should be angled inwards so the first few yards are run straight. The runner should accelerate as quickly as possible up to maximum speed which will be reached round about the 50 m mark. Up to this point all that has been said about 100 m applies equally to the 200 m. You should, however, even as early as this, strive for as much relaxation as is possible.

The Coast

After holding maximum speed for about 15 m the sprinter will begin to slow down. It is impossible to hold maximum speed for the whole of the race. By dropping tension and by building up strength and stamina it is possible to minimize the loss of speed over the last part of the race. The real secret of success lies in proper conditioning so that the athlete can stave off the effects of fatigue and finish strongly. The length of coast for the novice will vary between 100–120 m, but this is very much an individual matter and can be determined only by experience.

The Finish

The quality of the finish depends largely on the amount of work that the athlete has put in during the winter and early season. If he has developed strength and endurance a strong finish will come comparatively easily. He must guard against any tendency towards tension over the last part of the race, tuck the chin in a little and concentrate on the arm action. The best advice in a tight finish is to run straight through the tape to a point some 5 m beyond. A chest drop may be advantageous provided it can be timed correctly.

Bend Running

Nearly all 200 m races are run round a curve, the start being on the bend and the finish at the end of the straight. The standard differential between the race run on the straight and on the curve is 0·4 sec. It is, therefore, important to negotiate the bend skilfully, otherwise the differential will be considerably greater. The only way to become a good bend runner is by constant practice. The runner must lean in slightly and keep as close to the line as possible. The tighter the bend, the more lean that will be required. Practice with a rolling start over 110–150 m on an interval basis is the most satisfactory method of learning and training at the same time.

400 m

The quarter mile is a sustained sprint, maximum speed being reached about 60 m from the start. The runner holds top speed for a short period and then gradually slows up throughout the rest of the race, the fastest finisher being he who slows down least.

The Running Action

Basically the running action is the same as for the 100 m and 200 m but with less a powerful drive and slower rhythm for most of the race. The arms should be more relaxed and they should be held just a little lower during the middle part of the race. However, the athlete should concentrate on a powerful action of the arms to assist the legs over the last 50 m.

Although the knee lift is not so pronounced, stride length is held by the proper use of the hips in the running action. The latter will be obtained only by constant practice at speed and experience in competition. The ball of the foot will strike the ground first, the heel dropping low during the supporting phase although not actually making contact with the ground.

The secret of success in the race is to have built up a solid background of intelligent and well-planned conditioning work. Such a race requires all-the-year-round training of steadily increasing intensity. It is only in this manner that sufficient strength and endurance will be obtained to withstand the exacting demands of modern 400 m running.

Pace Judgement

The novice must find out what time to run his first 200 m; if he runs either too slow or too fast his overall time will suffer. He will be well advised to start by using the so-called British method where the first 200 m is run about 2 sec faster than the second 200 m. If the time of the race is going to be 54 sec then the first 200 m will be covered in 26 sec and the second 200 m in 28 sec, the 300 m being passed in 39·8 sec. However, most really fast races are fun with a considerably greater differential than this, often with as much as 4 sec between the two halves of the race. This approach to pace must come much later on in an athlete's career when he has gained experience and maturity. Even then he must be the right type of quarter miler, the sprinter coming up to 400 m. This type of runner must cover the first 200 m fast in order to take advantage of his speed before fatigue sets in.

Training Schedules: 100 m and 200 m

WINTER: OCTOBER–MARCH

Monday : Fartlek (5 miles)

Fast stretches interspersed with steady running and slow recovery jogs. This session should be carried out on grass if possible, but if it is impossible to use grass then on the roads from lamp-post to lamp-post. The fast stretches should vary from 60 m to 200 m.

Tuesday : Track

1. Warm-up (25 min) consisting of jogging, steady running and short wind sprints followed by suppling excercises with some emphasis on hip mobility.

2. $6 \times$ 300 m (42–45 sec) 5 min jog recovery.
3. Warm-down (10 min easy running on grass).

Wednesday : Fartlek (5 miles)

1. As on Monday.
2. Weight training or circuit training.

Thursday : Track

1. Warm-up (as shown on Tuesday).
2. 4×150 m (rest of lap jog recovery).
   5 min rest.
   4×150 m (rest of lap jog recovery).
   5 min rest.
   4×150 m (rest of lap jog recovery).
3. Warm-down (10 min easy running on grass).

Friday : Track

1. Warm-up (as before).
2. 6×200 m ($\frac{3}{4}$ effort) $3\frac{1}{2}$ min jog recovery.
   5 min rest.
   2×200 m ($\frac{7}{8}$ effort) $3\frac{1}{2}$ min jog recovery.
3. Warm-down (10 min easy running on grass).
4. Weight training or circuit training.

Saturday : Track

1. Warm-up (as before).
2. 10×60 m (full effort from blocks) walk back recovery.
3. Warm-down (as before).

Sunday : Track

1. Warm-up (as before).
2. 6×60 m (full effort from blocks) walk back recovery.
   5 min rest.
   4×80 m (full effort from blocks) $3\frac{1}{2}$ min recovery.

5 min rest.

2 × 150 m from blocks (full effort round bend) 5 min recovery.

APRIL–MAY

Monday

1. Warm-up (as before).
2. 1 × 300 m (full effort) 7 min recovery.
   6 × 80 m (full effort from blocks) $3\frac{1}{2}$ min recovery.
3. Warm-down (as before).
4. Weight training, isometric work or circuit training.

Tuesday

1. Warm-up (as before).
2. 6 × 60 m (full effort from blocks) walk back recovery.
   5 min rest.
   6 × 50 m (full effort from blocks) walk back recovery.

Wednesday

1. Warm-up (as before).
2. 5 × 150 m (full effort round bend) 5 min recovery.
   10 min rest.
   5 × 150 m (full effort round bend) 5 min recovery.
3. Warm-down (as before).
4. Weight training, isometric work or circuit training.

Thursday

1. Warm-up (as before).
2. Starting practice with the gun over 50 m. Occasionally put the finishing posts in and practise finishing.
3. Warm-down (as before).

Friday
Rest.

Saturday
Competition or time trail.

Sunday
6 × 60 m (full effort) walk back recovery.
5 min rest.
6 × 60 m (full effort) walk back recovery.

JUNE–AUGUST

Monday
1. Warm-up (as before)
2. 4 × 150 m (full effort) 5 min recovery.
   10 min rest.
   4 × 150 m (full effort) 5 min recovery.
3. Warm-down (10 min easy running on grass).

Tuesday
1. Warm-up (as before).
2. 6 × 60 m (full effort from blocks) walk back recovery.
   5 min rest.
   6 × 60 m (full effort from blocks) walk back recovery.
3. Warm-down (as before).

Wednesday
1. Warm-up (as before).
2. 1 × 150 m (full effort round bend) 5 min recovery.
   2 × 80 m (full effort from blocks) $3\frac{1}{2}$ min recovery.
   4 × 60 m (full effort from blocks) walk back recovery.

Thursday

1. Warm-up (as before).
2. Starts with the gun over 50 m.
3. Warm-down (as before).

Friday

Rest.

Saturday

Competition.

Sunday

Rest.

400 metres

WINTER: OCTOBER–MARCH

Monday: Fartlek (5 miles)

Fast stretches varying from 60 m to 300 m with short recovery jogs. Sprinting uphill and a certain amount of level pace running at approximately racing speed.

Tuesday

1. Warm-up (as before).
2. 6 × 200 m (at racing speed e.g. a 54 sec 400 m runner would run them in 27 sec). Take $3\frac{1}{2}$ min 400 m jog recovery between each fast stretch.
3. Warm-down (as before).

Wednesday

1. Warm-up (loosening and mobilizing work).

2. Weight training or circuit training.
3. Warm-down.

Thursday

1. Warm-up (as before).
2. 6 × 80 m (starting from blocks) walk back recovery.
   10 min rest.
   2 × 300 m at racing speed e.g. 200 m in 26 sec 300 m 39·8 sec for the 54 sec 400 m runner. Take 7 min recovery between the two runs.

Friday

Steady run from 3 to 5 miles. Preferably this should be done on grass but if necessary it will have to be carried out on the road. Weight training or circuit training afterwards.

Saturday

Cross-country run or fartlek as on Monday.

Sunday

1. Warm-up (as before).
2. 10 × 150 m (round the bend) jog rest of lap recovery.
3. Warm-down (as before).

APRIL–MAY

Monday

1. Warm-up (as before).
2. 4 × 200 m (26 sec) 5 min recovery. Speed for a 54 sec 400 m runner.
   10 min rest.
   6 × 60 m (full effort from blocks) walk back recovery.

3. Warm-down (as before).
4. Weight training, isometric work or circuit training.

Tuesday
1. Warm-up (as before).
2. 2 × 200 m (maximum effort) 5 min recovery.
   3 × 100m maximum effort) $3\frac{1}{2}$ min recovery.
   4 × 80 m (maximum effort from blocks) walk back recovery.
3. Warm-down (as before).

Wednesday
1. Warm-up (as before).
2. 10 × 150 m (maximum effort) $3\frac{1}{2}$ min recovery.
3. Warm-down (as before).
4. Weight training, isometric work or circuit training.

Thursday
1. Warm-up (as before).
2. 2 × 300 m (racing speed) 7 min recovery.
   10 min rest.
   4 × 80 m (full effort from blocks) $3\frac{1}{2}$ min recovery.
3. Warm-down (as before).

Friday
Rest.

Saturday
Competition or time trial.

Sunday
As Wednesday but without the progressive resistance work.

Monday

1. Warm-up (as before).
2. 4 × 200 m (25 sec) 5 min recovery. Speed for a 54 sec 400 m runner.
3. Warm-down (as before).

Tuesday

1. Warm-up (as before).
2. 4 × 150 m (maximum effort) $3\frac{1}{2}$ min recovery.
   7 min rest.
   4 × 150 m (maximum effort) $3\frac{1}{2}$ min recovery.
3. Warm-down (as before).

Wednesday

1. Warm-up (as before).
2. 2 × 300 m (maximum effort) 5 min recovery. 38·5 sec for a 54 sec 400 m runner.
   10 min rest.
   4 × 80 m (maximum effort from blocks) $3\frac{1}{2}$ min recovery.
3. Warm-down (as before).

Thursday

1. Warm-up (as before).
2. 10 × 60 m (maximum effort) walk back recovery.
3. Warm-down (as before).

Friday

Rest.

Saturday

Competition.

Sunday

Rest.

If you have the necessary apparatus, isometric work is an effective method of maintaining strength throughout the competitive season without the use of weights. This might be done on two evenings during the week and Sundays.

2. Middle-distance Running

The Running Action

There is little point in attempting to break down an individual running 'style'. This is something which has been developed since early childhood. The runner has, over the years, modified and corrected his limb movements instinctively to suit his physical characteristics. However, in all types of running there is a basic pattern of technique which you should follow in broad outline.

Arm Action

In running distance races the arms are used merely to balance the leg action. They should move from the shoulders with a natural easy swing towards the centre line of the body. There should be an angle of approximately 90 degrees between the upper and lower arm. However, there will very often be an opening out and closing of the arm as it swings. Provided this independent movement of the lower arm is not exaggerated, and balances the leg action, it should be left alone. Relaxation in the shoulders, wrists and fingers is important; normally the fingers should be lightly curled with the thumbs on top.

Leg Action

The cadence of the leg action is slowed down from that of sprinting and the knee lift is not so high. The runner is concerned with relaxation and ecconomy of effort rather than stride length or rate of striding. At the same time a sufficient stride length must be maintained. The important fundamentals of a good leg action are a relaxed free movement of the legs and the maintenance of sufficient range of movement from the hips.

At all costs avoid any tendency to attempt to increase stride length by reaching out in front with the foot of the recovery leg. It should be allowed to swing through easily, the foot coming just in front of the knee, and then hit the ground moving backwards. The ball of the foot should strike the ground first and as the body moves directly over the foot the heel should sink to the ground. This gives the calf muscles a momentary rest before the extension of the leg behind the body in the driving phase.

Body Lean

The forward lean of the body will be less than in sprinting. It is best not to worry too much about this aspect of the running action; the athlete will find that the forward lean of the body adjusts itself automatically to the details of his physique. He should, therefore, concentrate more on the correct action of the arms and legs and leave the body lean to take care of itself.

Tactics

Tactics and pace judgement go hand in hand; sound tactics will enable the runner to make the best use of his pace judgement. Tactical sense will develop as the athlete gains more experience and to this end he should attempt to learn from every race he runs. It is advisable for him to have a coach or knowledgeable friend watching his early races to help analyse his mistakes after the race.

The Start

It is advisable to get into a good position as early as possible in the race. To this end the first 200 m is usually run at a fast pace before the runners settle down to a regular pace for the middle part of the race. If the runner draws an outside position at the start, it is rarely a good thing for him to attempt to take the lead. This would mean the tremendous effort of running a greater distance at a much greater speed than the runners inside him at the start. In such a situation it is much wiser for him to work his way into a suitable position from behind and let the more favourably placed runners fight it out for the leading positions. It is recommended that a shorter stride and a slightly higher arm action are employed in this early hurly-burly jockeying for position.

The Middle of the Race

Tactically it is better to run either in second or third position during this part of the race. Most runners find it less tiring to follow than to lead and in second or third position a runner can, when necessary, take the lead. Running just off the shoulder of the leader is often a very good tactical position because it is possible to dictate, to a certain extent, how the race is to be run. If there is a challenge from behind, he can more easily fight it off; he may take the lead if he wishes and there is no likelihood of his being boxed in.

Passing

It is preferable to maintain an even pace throughout the middle part of the race and to avoid passing or fighting off a challenge. However, an opponent in front may slow up and in this case he must be passed, otherwise the leaders will open up a gap which may never be closed. When passing, it must be done briskly, accelerating rapidly from behind and the pressure continued for several yards beyond the opponent. If this passing movement is made sluggishly, without attack, the opponent may be encouraged to fight back; in this case it becomes a tussle which neither runner can afford. One should not pass on the bend unless it is absolutely necessary.

The Finish

It is a good thing if the runner puts in his finishing effort as early as possible in order to take advantage of the element of surprise. The athlete should be prepared to start his finishing burst any time after entering the back straight. He should take the lead here and avoid being passed on the back straight. At all costs, once the final effort has begun he must not weaken and change his mind. If the home straight is a long one, then it may be best to be off the leader's shoulder as he comes out of the bend. In this case he should accelerate rapidly up from behind as he comes out of the bend. The runner who takes the initiative at this point is very often the winner.

Training Schedules: 800/1500 metres

Most schoolboys and young middle-distance runners are concerned with both these distances and very often undecided which event they are best at or prefer. The following schedules are, therefore, planned to help the young athlete over this period and should produce good results at both distances.

Circuit training and/or weight training can be used with advantage in many cases as an addition to these training schedules. Circuit training might be the better alternative of the two for the middle-distance runner, but this depends largely on the requirements of the individual. However, never sacrifice a session of running for either weight training or circuit training. Strength may be obtained by running uphill, sandhill running or running over soft ground up gentle slopes.

WINTER: OCTOBER–MARCH

---

2 min 800 m 4 min 10 sec 1500 m

Monday: Fartlek (5–7 miles)
Preferably this should be carried out on grass but if neccesary the roads may have to be used.

Tuesday: Track
1. Warm-up steady running for 1500 m followed by excerises with some emphasis on hip mobility.
2. 8 × 400 m (66 sec) 400 m jog recovery.
3. Warm-down (800 m jogging).

Wednesday
Steady fartlek 5 miles.

Thursday: Track
1. Warm-up (as before).
2. 10 × 200 m (29 sec) 200 m jog recovery.
3. Warm-down (800 m jogging).

Friday
Rest

Saturday
Cross-country race.

Sunday: Track

1. Warm-up (as before).
2. 5 × 600 m (102 sec) 5 min jog recovery.
3. Warm-down (800 m jogging).

The times of the fast sections are only approximate and will vary with the individual. The important thing is to set yourself a target to work towards, gradually improving from month to month.

APRIL–MAY

Monday: Fartlek (5 miles).

Tuesday: Track

1. Warm-up (as before).
2. 8 × 400 m (63–64 sec) 400 m jog recovery.
3. Warm-down (800 jogging).

Wednesday: Track

1. Warm-up (as before).
2. 10 × 200 m (27 sec) 200 m jog recovery.
3. Warm-down (800 m jogging).

Thursday: Track

1. Warm-up (as before).
2. 12 × 150 m (maximum effort round bend) rest of lap jog recovery.
3. Warm-down (800 m jogging).

Friday

Rest

Saturday

Competition.

Sunday

5 miles steady run.

Monday : Fartlek (3–4 miles)

Tuesday

1. Warm-up (as before).
2. 4 × 400 m (62 sec) 400 m jog recovery.
   5 min rest.
   4 × 400 m (62 sec) 400 m jog recovery.
3. Warm-down (800 m jogging).

Wednesday

1. Warm-up (as before).
2. 6 × 200 m (26 sec) 200 m jog.
   5 min rest.
   6 × 200 m (26 sec) 200 m jog.
3. Warm-down (800 m jogging).

Thursday

1. Modified warm up.
2. 3 miles steady.
3. 6 × 150 m (full effort) rest of lap jog recovery.
4. Warm-down (800 m jogging).

Friday

Rest.

C

Saturday
Competition.

Sunday
Easy running or rest.

3 miles

WINTER: OCTOBER–MARCH

Monday
8 miles fast run on grass or road.

Tuesday
Fartlek (4–5 miles) or 6 mile road run.

Wednesday
1. Warm-up. Steady running for 1 mile followed by exercises with some emphasis on hip mobility.
2. 8×600 m with 400 m jog recovery. On track but if there is no track available, on grass.
3. Warm-down (3 lap jog).

Thursday
1. Warm-up (as before).
2. 6×1200 m (fast running) 800 m jog to recover. Either on track or on grass.

Friday
8–10 mile fartlek on grass.

Saturday
Cross-country run or race.

Sunday

8–10 miles steady on run grass.

Monday

1. Warm-up (as before).
2. 6 × 1200 m (400 m jog recovery).
3. Warm-down (3 lap jog).

Tuesday

1. Warm-up (as before)
2. 12 × 600 m (200 m jog recovery).
3. Warm-down (3 lap jog).

Wednesday

6 miles steady on grass.

Thursday

1. Warm-up (as before).
2. 4 × 400 m (100 m jog recovery).
   4 × 800 m (200 m jog recovery).
   4 × 400 m (100 m jog recovery).
3. Warm-down (3 lap jog).

Friday

Rest.

Saturday

Competition.

Sunday

7 miles fartlek.

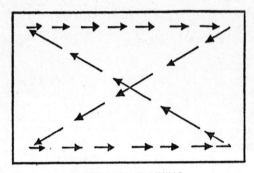

DIAGONAL RUNNING

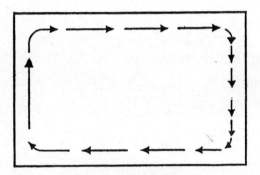

THREEQUARTER CIRCUITS

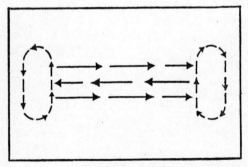

STRAIGHT 100's

Diagonal Running

The runner jogs along the top straight and then does a fast section diagonally across the field. He then jogs the bottom section and does another diagonal fast section to the corner from which he first started. This excercise should be carried out until the athlete feels he has had enough. From this beginning he should gradually increase the number of repetitions and speed as time goes on and fitness improves.

Threequarter Circuits

For the longer workouts three-quarters of the field is covered as the fast section and recovery is just a slow jog across the width of the field. This is an endurance workout and the fast sections will be slower than in diagonal running. Also the recovery periods are much shorter.

Straight 100's

A simple workout for speed on a field. A fast 100 m followed by a 30 sec. circular jog at the end of the field, returning straight up with another fast 100 m Repeat until tired.

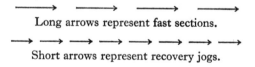

Long arrows represent fast sections.

Short arrows represent recovery jogs.

JUNE–AUGUST

Monday

1. Warm-up (as before).
2. 20 × 400 m (fast) 200 m jog 90 sec.
3. Warm-down (3 lap jog).

Tuesday

6 miles steady on grass.

Wednesday

1. Warm-up (as before).
2. 4 × 1200 m (400 jog recovery).
3. Warm-down (3 lap jog).

Thursday

Fartlek (5 miles on grass).

Friday

Rest.

Saturday

Competition.

Sunday

Fartlek (7 miles on grass).

The above schedules are to be used as a guide only to the young 3-miler. There are many methods by which you may achieve results in middle- and long-distance running. It depends largely on what facilities you have available and what type of work you like and suits you. Provided you mix speed and stamina work in the correct proportions at the right time and work hard, sucess will come.

Many athletes are faced with the problem of not having access to a floodlit track at night and have to be content with interval running at week-ends only. The layout shown in the diagrams illustrates simple workouts that can be carried out on fields provided they are reasonably level.

Planning the Competitive Season

Middle-distance, long-distance runners and steeplechasers should plan their competition carefully a soon as they know their racing commitments. The grammar school athlete will generally require two peaks, one in March–April and another in July–August. The young international should work to achieve one peak in June–July for the A.A.A. Championships and another later on in September–October for the major international championships such as the Olympic Games, European Championships and Commonwealth and Empire Games.

The exact time of these peaks will depend on the dates of the major competitions in the athlete's programme and the number of races on the plateau of each peak will depend to a large extent on the type of race. For example, the marathon runner will only want two or at the most three major races in the season. The short-middle-distance runner will probably find six seven or eight *really* fast races well within his capabilities. The season should be arranged with three or four of these races at each peak.

All other competition should be graduated carefully to work up to obtain maximum performances over the peak periods. During the week prior to each major effort the training load should be lightened in order to store up nervous energy for the race and during the last 48 hours before the race the work should be considerably lighter in order to allow the body to store up the carbohydrate which it requires for a major effort. In many cases the training schedules given in this book will have to be adjusted to suit these periods. There are so many factors involved that these fine adjustments can be worked out only by coach and athlete. It is crass folly to race blindly throughout the season attempting to achieve maximum performances in every race.

There is a happy medium in all these things. What has been dubbed in a derogatory manner in recent years 'the English method' of running—that is, running from behind and winning on a finishing burst—is obviously not good if it is the athlete's only way of running a race. It would be equal folly to attempt to

3. The Steeplechase

The best material for steeplechasing generally comes from the young cross-country runner who has also recorded a good time for the mile. He also needs to be the rugged, rangy type of runner who enjoys hard knocks and hard work. This country has wondeful material for this event; we have such an abundance of good middle-distance runners in the schools that it is a great pity that more of them are not channelled into steeplechasing.

It is sometimes useful to compare flat racing times with steeplechase times. The following is a list of comparable preformances as a rough guide:

2 mile flat time = 3000 metres steelpechase time.

3000 metres flat time + 35 sec = 3000 metres steeplechase time.

1 mile flat time = 1500 metres steeplechase time.

1500 metres flat time + 18 sec = 1500 metres steeplechase time.

400 m lap + 5 hurdles roughly equals 1 lap via water jump.

3000 metres steeplechase = $7\frac{1}{2}$ laps (28 hurdles and 7 water jumps).

2000 metres steeplechase = 5 laps (18 hurdles and 5 water jumps).

1500 metres steeplechase = $3\frac{3}{4}$ laps (13 hurdles and 3 water jumps).

Water Jump Clearance

The technique of water jumping can make a tremendous difference to the entire race. If the water jump is negotiated badly it can be very tiring indeed and in many cases cause the athlete to lose a race which he might have won.

Take-off

The take-off spot should fall between $4\frac{1}{2}$ ft–5 ft from the hurdle and depends largely on the speed of aproach of the athlete. As he nears the hurdle his speed should increase slightly in order to obtain a satisfactory clearance. A consistent take-off depends upon a reliable check mark some distance back from the hurdle. In the first instance one should try about 15 yd–16 yd away. This mark should be struck with the foot that the athlete wishes to put on the rail and this will give a seven-stride rhythm, the eighth stride landing on top of the hurdle.

Clearance

Generally the take-off foot for hurdling will be used on the hurdle rail. In other words it is better to use the stronger leg to push off from the rail. However, there may well be exceptions to this rule and, indeed, if the steeplechaser is weight training seriously, he will set about making himself strong in both legs. It is recommended that:

1. You should place the ball of your foot on the rail.
2. Your body should be lowered, as this leads to a smooth fast pivot in a crouched position on the rail.
3. Reach out well with the thigh of your leading leg off the hurdle.

4. You should keep pushing against the rail with the foot of your driving leg. This leads to a good split between the legs on landing.
5. Bring your trailing leg through high to avoid any tendency to stumble and to keep the running action going.
6. It is preferable for you to land in about 6 in. of water and, therefore, step out of the water on your first stride. This generally means that you will only get one foot wet during the race. However, through lack of strength and endurance you may find you have to drop short and run out as best you can.

Tactics

If the pace is fast it is advisable to stay back out of trouble and take the first obstacle behind the main bunch. You should now work your way through the field gradually as they string out. If you make body contact with another runner during either the water jump or hurdle clearances it may well prove disastrous to your chance of winning the race.

On the other hand, if the pace is slow, then take advantage of the first 240 m or so without an obstacle and get clear of the field. In this way you may take the first obstacle safely without any chance of interference. Never approach the water jump or a hurdle directly behind another runner. You may find it helpful tactically to place your check mark for the water jump three strides from take-off. This means your mark is clearly defined away from the main ruck of marks on the ground and you may accelerate past other runners on to your mark closer in. If you can master this technique and approach the jump with confidence you will find it extremely helpful. This method was devised and used by Chris Brasher (Olympic Champion 1956) with great success.

Hurdle Clearance

It is vitally important for the steeplechaser to become a good hurdler. Jumping, as opposed to *running* over the hurdles, takes up a tremendous amount of energy and not only does it mean a poor hurdle clearance but also leads to a bad landing and the effort of accelerating again on the far side of the obstacle. The athlete cannot afford to make mistakes because the hurdles will not fall over, the jostling of other competitors makes hurdling difficult and sometimes dangerous and he has to face hurdles when extremely tired. All this means he has to hurdle well if only to keep himself out of trouble.

Take off

1. The take-off spot depends largely on the speed at which you approach the hurdle. A rough guide would be about 6 ft away, but this may get in as close 5 ft 6 in.
2. Keep as near as you can to a level pace because this will help consolidate your take-off spot. Speed up the same amount each time you approach a hurdle—this emphasizes the importance of interval hurdling. It is not sufficient, especially in the early days of your training, to carry out interval running and hurdling as separate activities.
3. Learn to judge the hurdles correctly. Keep your eyes on each hurdle as you approach it; it is a great temptation to drop the head as you tire towards the end of the race.
4. In training it is a good idea for you to get used to taking hurdles at varying speeds. You may find this stands you in good stead at a critical time during a race.
5. Do not stutter before the hurdle; keep the stride going at all costs.

Crossing the Hurdle

1. You should study the form of the 400 m hurdler and modify his technique to suit the speed of the race.
2. Attempt to clear the hurdles without any wasted effort.
3. Your leading leg should be picked up fast and body dip begin before you break contact with the ground.
4. The leading arm should go out and down as you rise to the hurdle. This, with adequate body dip will keep your shoulders square to the front and help you to come off the hurdle with an easy running action.
5. As you come off the hurdle, the trailing leg should be brought through late but fast.

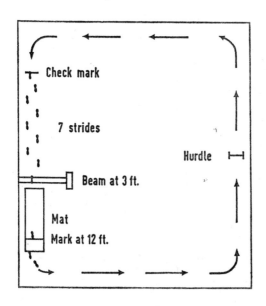

Training

As an adjunct to your interval running and interval hurdling, indoor hurdling and water-jump practice may be carried out once or twice a week in a gymnasium.

Gymnasium work (one or two days per week).

1. Warm-up (20 min). Consisting of running, suppling, stretching and mobilizing exercises. Follow this by a few minutes' hurdle stepping.
2. Skills. Water-jump practice and hurdle clearance doing circuits of the gymnasium as shown in the diagram. This can be done either as one excerise or in sets of so many laps of the gymnasium with a short rest between sets (20 min).
3. Weight training (as shown under weight training).
4. Warm-down (10 min). Jogging and light excerises.

Occasionally it is advisable to vary this and put the skills practice in after the weight training or do another session of skills (10 min) afterwards.

Training Schedules

In the early days of a steeplechaser's career he should do a considerable amount of interval hurdling at varying distances. Sessions with five hurdles in position on the 400 m circuit should take place on two or three days each week. In this way he learns the pattern of the race and acquires the ability to take each hurdle smoothly when his senses are dulled by fatigue.

He should build up the race step by step by occasionally doing a given number of laps in his racing target time. The number of laps should gradually be increased as strength and fitness improve. In this way confidence is installed into the runner and he finds himself able to go into competition with the aggressive determination to win. Fartlek, fell running and mountain climbs could play an important part in building up the necessary physical and mental fitness for this strenuous event.

WINTER: OCTOBER—MARCH

3000 metres Steeplechase. Target Time 9·0 min

Monday

1. Warm-up 1 mile steady running followed by exercises with some emphasis on hip mobility.
2. 12 × 400 m (65) 400 m jog recovery.
3. Warm-down (800 m jogging).

Tuesday

1. Warm-up (as before)
2. 3–4 laps to a 9·0 min scedule.
   3 laps in 4 min 11 sec.
   4 laps in 5 min 23 sec.
   Start with three laps and gradually increase month by month Allow 35 sec or more for the run to the first hurdle depending on whether you are working to a track either 6 yd or 10 yd short via the water jump. This workout may have to be adjusted to running over five hurdles if the water jump is not in use or unsatisfactory.
3. Warm-down (800 m jogging).

Wednesday

Weight training and gymnasium work as previously outlined. This should take place on two or three nights per week and should be fitted into the schedule as suits the convenience of the athlete. In some cases this may mean training twice in one day.

On these occasions the first workout should be comparatively light.

Thursday
1. Warm-up (as before).
2. 10 × 400 m (five hurdles in position) 400 m jog recovery.
3. Warm-down (800 m jogging).

Friday
Repeat Wednesday's workout.

Saturday
Cross-country race.

Sunday
Repeat Monday's workout or fartlek (5 miles).

A typical weight-training schedule should include:
1. *Step-ups* on to a 20 in. bench. Start at 80 lb on the bar doing three sets of eight repetitions.
2. *Cheat press:* 3 × 6 repetitions.
3. *Abdominal:* 2 × 10 repetitions with 10 lb disc.
4. *Clean and jerk:* 3 × 4 repetitions starting with a light weight and gradually progressing as the skill becomes easier.
5. *Toe pushing:* 2 × 20 lb at 80 lb. Toes resting on a 3 in. ledge with the bar across the shoulders. Extend the ankles and lower the heels to the ground.

APRIL–MAY

Weight training may be continued on one or two days per week during this period. However, some steeplechasers may prefer to substitute hard interval running and hurdling at this stage in

48

order to make up for time they have lost during the winter months. The type of work you do will depend largely on the facilities you have at your disposal and the work you have carried out during the out-of-season period. You should consult your coach who will have a detailed knowledge of your requirements.

Monday

1. Warm-up 1 mile steady running followed by exercises with some emphasis on hip mobility.
2. 12 × 400 m (63) 400 m jog recovery.
3. Warm-down (800 m jogging).

Tuesday (once a fortnight)

1st Week

1. Warm-up (as before).
2. Four–five laps to a 9 min schedule.
   Four laps in 5 min 23 sec.
   Five laps in 6 min 35 sec.
   This workout may have to be adjusted to running over 5 hurdles if the water jump is not in use or unsatisfactory.
3. Warm-down (800 m jogging).

2nd Week

For the second week substitute:

1. Warm-up (as before).
2. 6 × 800 m (approximately 2 min 10 sec) two laps jog recovery.
3. Warm-down (800 m jogging).

Wednesday

1. Warm-up (as before).
2. 5 × 800 m with five hurdles (2 min 18 sec) 5 min recovery.
3. Warm-down (800 m jogging).

Thursday

1. Warm-down (as before).
2. 10 × 300 m (45) 2½ min jog recovery.
3. Warm-down (800 m jogging).

Friday

Rest

Saturday

Competition.

Sunday

Fartlek (5–6 miles).

JUNE–AUGUST

Monday

1. Warm-up (as before).
2. 10 × 400 m (62) 400 jog recovery.
3. Warm-down (800 jogging).

Tuesday

1. Warm-up (as before).
2. 3 × 1200 m with five hurdles (3.30) 10 min recovery.
3. Warm-down (800 m jogging).

Wednesday

1. Warm-up (as before).
2. 8 × 400 m with hurdles (66) 3½ min jog recovery.
3. Warm-down (800 m jogging).

Thursday

1. Warm-up (as before).

2. 15 × 200 m (28) 200 m jog recovery.
3. Warm-down (800 jogging).

Friday
Rest.

Saturday
Competition.

Sunday
Long steady run, 7–8 miles.

The author would like to point out that training for the steeplechase, as for middle- and long-distance running, is a highly individual matter. These schedules are only a guide to the comparative novice and are not laid down as the one specific road to success. If you base your training along these lines you will not go far wrong, but remember you are an individual and as you gain experience and strength you must devise your own variation of this method.

4. Hurdles

Basically hurdling is a sprint event with obstacles to be cleared with the greatest possible speed and with as little interruption to the normal running action as possible. This requires certain modifications to the sprinting action on each clearance stride, and since the hurdles are 3 ft 6 in. high this is not easy. The hurdler, therefore, requires qualities of speed, flexibility, co-ordination and length of leg which only a few men possess.

Most hurdlers are 6 ft in height or over; however, a man of 5 ft 10 in. with long legs will be able to manage high hurdles provided he possesses the other qualities needed to become a hurdler. Flexibility is a vital factor in this event, particularly in the hips and spine. The loose-limbed individual will find hurdle clearance less exacting. Co-ordination of the body movement and concentration are the 'Roland & Oliver' of competition in this event, the co-ordination required to perform the highly skilled movement across the hurdles and the concentration to be able to perform it ten times in the race without even a slight mistake which might spell disaster. It is as well to remember, at this stage, that concentration in training is much easier than concentration in competition. In competition the athlete has men on either side of him and the inexperienced hurdler is liable to be distracted and even tend to pick up their rhythm. Therefore, the young hurdler must obtain as much competition as he can and not be put off by setbacks early in his career.

The Start.

The hurdler should employ a normal medium-type start as described in the chapter on sprinting. However, certain modifications may have to be made to the opening strides to fit in with the stride plan to the first hurdle. It must be borne in mind that there is a tremendous advantage in reaching the first hurdle before the other competitors. Hence much practice must be carried out on this phase of the race. Many young hurdlers spend so much time on hurdle clearance in training that they forget about the approach to the first obstacle and and speed in between the hurdles.

Stride Plan

The normal hurdler will find that eight strides to the first hurdle (clearing on the ninth) is the most suitable arrangement. However, some tall men or long-striding individuals may find that seven strides (clearing on the eighth) suits them better. In this case it is as well to remember that there will be difficulty in breaking down to a shorter and faster striking rhythm in between the following hurdles. Therefore, it is folly to practise a seven-stride approach only clearing the first obstacle. At least three hurdles should be used and the athlete must continue to concentrate on speed over the last two hurdles. If the eight-stride plan is being used, then the athlete must start with the foot back on the starting position with which he wishes to lead over the hurdle.

Clearance

Total distance taken up in clearing the hurdle will be approximately 11 ft, the hurdler taking off about 7 ft away from the hurdle and landing about 4 ft away on the far side. The take-off is further away in order to give time to get the leading leg up. The faster the athlete is moving towards the hurdle, the further back he has to take off unless he can get his lead leg up faster still.

Leading Leg

A fast leading leg is the panacea of hurdling. In many cases a hurdler who is not quite 'hitting it off' can be transformed by speeding up the action of the lead leg, the knee should be brought up bent and fast and the foot thrown at the hurdle rail. A sluggish lead leg produces a sitting position on top of the hurdle. A fast lead leg gives a wide split between the thighs on the take-off side of the hurdle. Then, as the athlete crosses the hurdle, the trail leg will come through late but fast. The classic example of a good 'split' was Dick Attesley (USA) who had legs below the hurdle on either side as he cleared.

Trailing Leg

The trailing leg should not be delayed in order to produce a 'split' over the hurdle but rather should the lead leg be brought up faster. The trailing leg should start to come through as the lead leg goes down across the hurdle. The thigh of the trailing leg should be swept through into the first stride on landing. On the take-off side of the hurdle, the athlete should think of picking the lead leg up fast and on the far side of the hurdle he should think of pulling the trailing leg through fast.

Body-dip

Body-dip must begin before the hurdler breaks contact with the ground. In order to facilitate a lean at this stage, the last stride before the hurdle should be shortened fractionally; this will pitch the hurdler *at* and *across* the hurdle. He will now be taking off with forward rotation in the body and will tend to spin to the ground about a tranverse axis which passes through his centre of gravity. As he crosses the hurdle, the chest should lie along the thigh of the leading leg and the shoulders must remain square to the front. Adequate body-dip at take-off will ensure that the hurdler comes off each hurdle in a running position and that there is no twist back of the shoulders in reaction to the wide sweep-through of the trailing leg.

Position of the Head

Since the head tends to act as a rudder to the body in this type of movement, its position throughout the hurdle clearance is of the utmost importance. The beginner and even most of the accomplished hurdlers will keep the head up during clearance, the eyes being focussed down the flight of hurdles. However, some great hurdlers drop the head and look down towards the leading knee during clearance in order to produce more body-dip. The beginner is not advised to attempt this technique because he will find it difficult to maintain balance on landing. He would be better advised to make himself so supple while he is young that he can produce adequate body-dip without having to resort to dropping the head.

Arm action

The novice (and, indeed, the majority of hurdlers) is best advised to concentrate on an orthodox single-arm action unless, of course, there is a specific reason for utilizing a double-arm shifter. The double-arm action does help keep the shoulders square to the front, increase body-dip and, in the case of a very tall athlete, assist in shortening his first stride on landing.

The opposite arm to the leading leg should be moved fast out and down to assist the action of the leading leg. The shoulder should be pushed in as well; this with body-dip will keep the shoulder square on landing and assist in maintaining the sprinting action off the hurdle. The arm, having gone out and down to begin with, will now swing back and round in counteraction to the trailing leg sweeping through.

The Run-in

The last 15 yd from the tenth hurdle to the tape very often decide the outcome of a race. The majority of hurdlers take just over six strides to cover the distance from the last hurdle to the finish. If the foot lands just short of the line on the completion of the last stride, then a 'drop' finish might be employed with advantage. However, it is clearly best for the beginner to concentrate on maintaining a correct sprinting action right through the tape to a point some yards beyond. In training it is best to insert finishing posts and a line at the correct distance and practise the finish when training over three, four or five hurdles.

Learning to Hurdle

1. You should obtain the guidance of a qualified teacher of physical education in the preparation of a table of suppling and mobilizing exercises appertaining to hurdling; these might include the following:

(a) *The three right-angles position on the ground.* From this position do various trunk movements such as pressing forwards and down with the hand of the leading arm coming in line and to the side of the forward foot. Without using the hands lift the body and turn so that the other leg is forward. Now you should repeat the exercises.

(b) Place the heel of your lead leg on the hurdle rail. Grasp the hurdle with both hands about shoulder width apart and work the trailing (supporting) leg backwards until you are in a 'splits' position. Now bounce the hips rhythmically up

(c) Placing your trailing leg on the hurdle rail (foot and knee), bend down with rhythmic movements to touch the ground (with the hand of the leaning (inside) arm) close to the foot of the supporting (leading) leg.

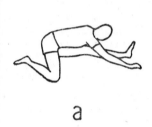

a

b

c

d

and down. It is best to have a companion supporting the hurdle while carrying out this exercise.

(d) Lean forward and grasp a wall bar or similar support with both hands shoulder width apart. Move the supporting (leading) leg back a bit so there is considerable forward lean of the trunk. Now work your trailing leg from the hip in a rotary action as in hurdle clearance. Emphasize the lift of the thigh, knee and foot being kept parallel to the ground as the leg is swept through.

You will require about half a dozen such exercises and these should be carried out daily. Mobilizing work is so important to you, right from an early age, that you must enlist the help of a specialist in physical education. The above exercises are only just an indication of the type of work that may be done.

2. You may learn to hurdle indoors during the winter months. Start by setting up two very low hurdles in a gymnasium at a suitable distance for taking three strides in between, with four strides clearing on the fifth to the first hurdle. You should practise sprinting over these obstacles with as little interruption to the normal running action as possible.

3. Raise the height of the hurdles as you become more proficient. As the height of obstacles increases so will your take-off go further back in order to give time to get your leading leg up. Your running action must now be modified by bringing the trailing leg round to the side. The arm action and body-dip must also be more pronounced.

4. If you find it difficult to obtain body dip then place the high jump stands on either side of the hurdle with the bar at your standing height. Now hurdle going underneath the bar and over the hurdle. Later bring the stands and bar about 6 in. on the take-off side of the hurdle, this will encourage you to

start your body-dip early. In the early stages of this exercise it might be advisable for you to have the bar at about 2 in. above your standing height.

5. Exercises, hurdle pivoting, mobilizing work and progressive resistance training should be continued indoors either before or after your hurdling practice.

6. As soon as the weather permits go outside and put up three to five hurdles at the correct height and distance apart. A cinder strip will do for this workout. Grass is quite unsatisfactory and can be dangerous when wet.

Training: 110 metres High Hurdles

OCTOBER–MARCH

This is the time when the novice must learn the basic skills of the event. He must put in a lot of practice both indoors in a gymnasium over two hurdles and on the track whenever possible over three, four and five hurdles. Later on, an occasional run over a full flight will be necessary in order to give him confidence. Even the experienced hurdler must do some technique work during the winter. He should work indoors and at least twice a week on the track.

Basic fitness must be built up with interval running, mobilizing exercises must be done regularly and weight training for strength three times a week. Isometric work may be done once per week instead of one night's weight training if this is preferred. Much of the hurdler's training may be done with the sprinter's such as short interval running and sprint starting.

A typical winter schedule might go something like this:

continued on page 62

59

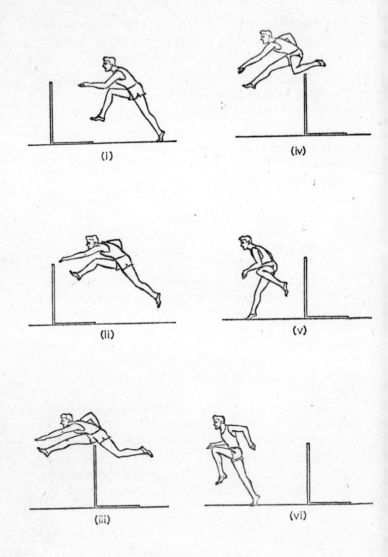

(i)

(iv)

(ii)

(v)

(iii)

(vi)

(i) There is a marked forward lean of the body at take-off and the opposite arm is moving rapidly out and down. The thigh of the leading leg has been picked up rapidly. In general the picture illustrates the athlete driving at and across the hurdle.

(ii) The chest now lies along the thigh of the leading leg and the opposite arm is well forward slightly above and to the left of the right foot. The heel of the lead leg (right leg) is being directed at the hurdle rail. This is the beginning of the 'splits' position.

(iii) The leading leg is now going down on the far side of the hurdle and the trailing leg will come through rapidly in reaction to the fast pick-up of the leading leg. Note that the left arm and shoulder are still well forward at this stage.

(iv) The athlete is now in the middle of the pivoting action over the hurdle. As the leading leg continues downwards towards the ground (on no account must it be deliberately swept *back* and down) so the trailing (left) leg is swept round and through with the knee and foot parallel to the hurdle. The toes of the left foot should be cocked up at the point to avoid hitting the hurdle rail. The athlete will find it helpful to think of pulling the toes forward and at the same time the foot will automatically rise in relation to the ankle.

(v) The hurdler has now landed some 4 ft away on the far side of the hurdle. Note that he has come down running and the shoulders remain square to the front.

(vi) The left leg has been swept through into the first stride and he is back into his sprinting action without any embarrassing twist back of the shoulders brought about by having insufficient body-dip to minimize the normal reaction of the shoulders to the wide rotary action of the bent trailing leg.

Monday : Gymnasium

1. Mobilizing exercises.
2. Work over 2 hurdles (20 min).
3. Weight training (30 min).
4. Warm-down.

Tuesday : Track

1. Warm-up consisting of jogging, steady running and short wind sprints followed by mobilizing exercises and hurdle stepping.
2. 12 × 3 hurdles with full run-in past a finishing post.
3. 2 × 150 m (full effort) $3\frac{1}{2}$ min recovery.
4. Warm-down (10 min easy running on grass).

Wednesday : Gymnasium

As Monday.

Thursday : Track

1. Warm-up (as before).
2. 10 × 60 m (full effort from blocks) walk back recovery.
3. Warm-down (as before).

Friday : Gymnasium

As Monday and Tuesday.

Saturday : Track

1. Warm-up (as before).
2. 8 × 4 hurdles with full run in past finishing post.
3. Warm-down (as before).

Sunday

Rest—mobilizing exercises.

Sessions of fartlek may be substituted if facilities are not available on certain nights.

APRIL–MAY

Monday : Gymnasium
1. Mobilizing exercises.
2. Work over 2 hurdles (20 min).
3. Weight training (30 min).
4. Warm-down.

Tuesday : Track
1. Warm-up (as before).
2. 8 × 5 hurdles with full run-in, take 4 min recovery between runs.
3. Warm-down (as before).

Wednesday : Track
1. Warm-up (as before).
2. Sprint starts with the sprinters (10 min).
3. 4 × 80 m (from blocks) walk back recovery.
4. Isometric work or light weight training (20 min).
5. Warm-down (as before).

Thursday
1. Mobilizing exercises (10 min).
2. Light sprinting (15 min).
3. Hurdle stepping (10 min).
4. Warm-down (as before).

Friday
Rest.

Saturday
Competition.

Sunday

Rest.

Monday

1. Warm-up (as before).
2. Work over two hurdles for technique. Correction of any faults shown in Saturday's competition.
3. Weight training.
4. Warm-down (as before).

Tueday

1. Warm-up (as before).
2. A few starts and runs over five or six hurdles.
3. Warm-down (as before).

Wednesday

1. Warm-up (as before).
2. 8 × 60 m (from blocks at maximum effort) walk back recovery.
3. Isometric work or light weight training.
4. Warm-down (as before).

Thursday

1. Warm-up (as before).
2. Sprint starts with the sprinters.
3. Hurdle stepping (10 min).
4. Warm-down (as before).

Friday

Rest.

Saturday
Competition.

Sunday
Rest.

Weight Training for Hurdling

As a guide to the hurdler the following schedule will be of some help. The beginner is advised to enlist the assistance of a physical educational specialist if he has done no weight training previously.

1. *Alternate Dumbell Press:* 5 sets of 6 repetitions at 30 lb.
2. *Abdominal Raise:* 2 sets of 10 repetitions at 20 lb.
3. *Clean and Jerk:* 4 sets of 6 repetitions at 100 lb.
4. *Squat or Straddle Lift:* 4 sets of 5 repetitions at 180 lb.

The poundage mentioned should not necessarily be copied, the weight is included only as an example. Handle the maximum possible to complete each exercise.

400 m Intermediate Hurdles

The 400 m hurdles is an event that requires qualities of speed, endurance and determination. The prospective 400 m hurdler must be capable of a very good time over the flat distance and also have the endurance to produce a useful time over 800 m. T. S. Farrell, who was our best 400 m hurdler prior to the Olympic Games in Rome 1960, switched to the 800 m during the winter of 1956–60 and that season won the A.A.A. 800 m title and went on to represent Great Britain in the 800 metres in the Olympic Games.

The technique of this event is roughly between that of the

E

100 m high hurdles and the 200 m low hurdles but with a slower pivot over the hurdle than in the other races. The 400 m race demands economy of effort in hurdle clearance and striding between the hurdles. Fast times will be achieved only when a fast economical stride has been developed and the athlete has the stamina to maintain it throughout the race.

Approach to the First Hurdle

The distance from the starting line to the first hurdle is 49¼ yd, therefore it is hard to lay down an exact number of strides for the athlete to take to the first obstacle. However, twenty-three strides would be average but this might vary between twenty-two and twenty-four depending upon the physique of the athlete and the length of his opening strides. Once the number of strides has been decided upon the start and pick-up to the first hurdle must be consolidated by constant practice until the hurdler can hit the same spot for take-off with absolute consistency.

Hurdle Clearance

There are several advantages in having a left leg lead in this event. Hurdling on the bends is very much easier with the left leg leading, the rotary action of the right leg tends to pull the athlete in and the right arm can be thrown slightly across towards the left foot. A right leg lead means running an extra 3 m in the race since the hurdler must run towards the outside of his lane to avoid fouling with the trailing (left) leg. Also since he has to lean in when cornering he must possess extreme flexibility in the left hip in order to pull the trailing leg through parallel to the hurdle rail. Finally, the rotary acton of the left leg tends to pull the athlete out from the line as it comes through into the first stride on landing. For these reasons it is best for the athlete to master a left leg lead early on in his career.

Since the race is run in echelon, he must learn to negotiate the hurdles in all the lanes in order to master the art of clearing the hurdles on a tight bend as well as on the wide curve of the outside lane.

The pattern of movement over the hurdles is similar to that shown in the high hurdles except that the hurdles being 3 ft instead of 3 ft 6 in., the amount of body-dip and hip flexibility required is less. The pivot over the hurdle is slower and more in keeping with the speed of the 400 m than the very fast pivot employed by the 110 m hurdler.

Strides between Hurdles

The majority of young hurdlers will find that fifteen strides between hurdles suits them best. This will mean an average stride length of slightly over 7 ft in order to hold this stride plan for the entire race. Many athletes, when tiring over the last part of the race, will drop to seventeen strides for the last few clearances. The effectiveness of this method depends on the smoothness with which the transition from fifteen to seventeen strides is obtained. The hurdler must know at what point he is going to make the change and adjust his strides coming off the previous hurdle—in this way no speed is lost. The athlete who suddenly realizes, as he approaches the seventh hurdle, that he is not going to make it in fifteen strides and then has to stutter prior to take-off has lost both speed and rhythm. Some powerful long-striding athletes have managed a thirteen-stride plan between and again others have alternated for part of the race taking fourteen strides. Whatever plan the beginner decides on he must perfect it quickly. Correct striding between hurdles is the key to success in this event.

67

The Finish

The last hurdle and run-in are of great importance because the race is often lost through lack of strength and endurance. The hurdler arriving at the last obstacle in a state of exhaustion somehow has to find reserves of mental and physical strength to clear the hurdle and maintain his rate of striding over the last $46\frac{1}{2}$ yd to the tape. A sprint finish is virtually impossible if the race has been run correctly; even the world's greatest 400 m hurdlers, in a hard-run race, are only in a fit state to hold on to their length of stride and cadence at this stage.

Training Schedules for the 400 m Hurdles

OCTOBER–MARCH

As with the other hurdling events this is the time for the novice to groove in the technique of the event. Some work can be done in the gymnasium over two hurdles and, of course, mobilizing exercises should be done daily. Weight training and isometric work should also be done in order to produce the necessary physical strength for this most exacting event. Many men have reached the top without the help of weight training but in these days of highly intensive competition the athlete is best advised to take advantage of every training aid. In order to win under the stress imposed when the athlete has become an ambassador of his country and more than just the honour and glory hangs in the balance, the modern athlete cannot afford to have one weak link in his armour.

A typical schedule for this period:

Monday: Gymnasium

1. Mobilizing exercises.

2. Work over two hurdles (20 min).
3. Weight training (30 min).
4. Warm-down.

Tuesday : Track

1. Warm-up consisting of jogging, steady running and short wind sprints followed by mobilizing exercises and hurdle stepping.
2. 8 × 400 m (64 sec) 400 m jog recovery.
3. Warm-down (10 min easy running on grass).

Wednesday : Gymnasium

As Monday.

Thursday : Track

1. Warm-up (as before).
2. Five or six runs over five hurdles correctly spaced. In this exercise top-class hurdlers will be taking approximately 4 sec from the top of one hurdle to the top of the next. Attention should be paid to the stride plan to the first hurdle and also between hurdles. Keep the recovery as short as possible.
3. Warm-down (as before).

Friday : Gymnasium

As Monday and Tuesday.

Saturday : Track

1. Warm-up (as before).
2. 220 m (maximum effort) 200 m jog recovery.
   7 min rest.
   4 × 200 m (maximum effort) 200 m jog recovery.
3. Warm-down (as before).

Sunday

Rest and mobilizing exercises.

Sessions of 5–3 miles fartlek may be substituted if facilities are not available on certain nights.

APRIL–MAY

Monday: Gymnasium

1. Mobilizing exercises.
2. Work over two hurdles (20 min).
3. Weight training (30 min).
4. Warm-down (as before).

Tuesday: Track

1. Warm-up (as before).
2. 6 runs over five hurdles correctly spaced keeping the recovery as short as possible. Occasionally run over six or seven hurdles towards the end of the workout to get used to taking more hurdles when tired.
3. Warm-down (as before).

Wednesday

1. Warm-up (as before).
2. 6 × 300 m (38–40 sec) 5 min recovery.
3. Weight training or isometric work.
4. Warm-down (as before).

Thursday

1. Warm-up (as before).
2. Hurdle stepping (10 min).
3. Starting practice with the sprinters (15 min).
4. 3 × 200 m with two hurdles the correct distance apart with

the correct run-in at the end of the 220 m. Take 5 min recovery between the three repetitions.

Friday

Rest.

Saturday

Competiton.

Sunday

Rest.

JUNE–AUGUST

Monday

1. Warm-up (as before).
2. Five runs over five hurdles correctly spaced with full run-in to finish.
3. Weight training.
4. Warm-down (as before).

Tuesday

1. Warm-up (as before).
2. 6 × 300 m (38 sec) 5 min recovery.
3. Warm-down (as before).

Wednesday

1. Warm-up (as before).
2. 4 × 200 m at 1 sec slower than fastest 200 m time. Take 5 min recovery between runs.
3. Isometric work or weight training.
4. Warm-down (as before).

Thursday

1. Warm-up (as before).
2. Sprint starts with the sprinters.
3. 3 × 150 m (maximum effort) $3\frac{1}{2}$ min recovery.
4. Hurdle stepping (10 min).
5. Warm-down (as before).

Friday

Rest.

Saturday

Competition.

Sunday

Rest.

5. The High Jump

The world's greatest high jumpers are now employing either the Straddle technique or the Fosbury Flop. Because of its simplicity many high jumpers have found the Fosbury Flop method has suited them admirably and they have achieved heights which have eluded them before. Others starting with the Fosbury, as a natural progression from the Scissor technique, have achieved good results very rapidly. However, Straddle jumpers still dominate the men's event because it is the most sophisticated of all techniques.

The only real problem with the Fosbury method is one of facilities. It is essential that jumpers have a suitable landing area, large enough and deep enough to ensure safety when landing on the back. This means that the ends of the area must extend on either side of the uprights and go far enough back to prevent the jumper rolling off and striking the ground. The first part of this text deals with the Straddle technique in some detail and the last part with pictures of Cornelia Popescu demonstrating an excellent Fosbury Flop.

No matter what technique the jumper employs in bar clearance, it must be remembered that by far the most important factor in jumping for height lies in a long period of basic conditioning. This will include specific work to increase strength and mobility and a series of specific excerises directed towards improving the jumper's technical ability. If these important aspects are neglected then the young high jumper can never achieve his true potential.

The Straddle

Approach

Most beginners tend to run both too far and too fast as they approach the bar. If this is the case, the jumping leg tends to buckle and the efficiency of the take-off is impaired. It is better, therefore, in the early days of a jumper's career to employ a short run-up of five or seven strides. However, as his technique and strength improve over the years, he should experiment with a longer, faster run and learn to handle the greater speed to his best advantage at the take-off. It matters little whether the jumper uses an odd or even number of strides in the run-up. There is a slight advantage in utilizing the odd number merely because you may start the run, hit the check mark and take-off spot all with the same foot.

During the first few strides of the approach, the upper body is tilted forward; the last three strides are accelerating ones during which the jumper prepares himself for the spring by lowering the hips and getting them ahead of the shoulders. The degree of backward lean employed by each jumper will vary considerably and will depend on the speed of approach, type of free leg swing, strength of the jumping leg and the ability to co-ordinate his movements correctly.

Direction

The angle of approach for the Straddle will vary between 25 degrees and 40 degrees. The world's greatest jumpers employ run-ups which are generally longer, faster and more acute than ever before. Brumel (U.S.S.R.) 25 degrees, Petterson (Sweden) 25 degrees, Shavlakadze (U.S.S.R.) 25 degrees. The beginner using a comparatively slow run should approach the bar at an angle varying between 30 degrees and 40 degrees.

Take-off

This is the most important part of high jumping technique; form in the air is of secondary importance to an effective take-off. The main concern of the jumper should be improvement in all departments of the jump prior to breaking contact with the ground. At this point it must be remembered that technique and strength go hand in hand and it is of little use attempting to make drastic improvements in this department unless the jumper is at the same time building-up all-round bodily strength. Particular attention should be paid to the legs, hips and abdomen.

The jumping foot should be planted well in front of the body weight and the athlete should be in a position of extreme backward lean. The heel of the jumping foot will have contacted the ground well in advance of the ball of the foot—heel spikes are therefore a necessity. The non-jumping leg, which has been trailing, now begins its swing from the hip with the knee bent in order to avoid striking the ground. Many high jumpers prefer to have a flat shoe or no shoe at all on the free leg in case the spikes should catch the ground. As soon as the foot has passed in front of the body, the leg straightens at the knee, the jumper striving to obtain the greatest possible speed of swing as the leg passes through the horizontal position.

Many jumpers find it impossible to employ a straight free leg swing and have to be content with the greatest possible speed with a bent leg. This is not so satisfactory for several reasons but, nevertheless, jumpers have cleared heights in excess of 7 ft with this method. The novice may have to be content with a bent free leg swing to start with but throughout the early years of his career should attempt to improve by mastering a higher, straighter and faster swing.

Quite a large number of champions nowadays manage to

use both arms in the upward swing at take-off in order to gain extra momentum. In this case both arms must be taken back behind the body on the penultimate stride at the same time as the hips are sinking. Most novices can only manage an effective swing of one arm, the opposite one to the free leg, the inside shoulder being hunched at the same time. These are, of course the arm and shoulder nearest to the bar.

In order to ascertain his take-off spot, the jumper should stand along the line of his approach facing along the bar; for a left-footed jumper this means facing to the right. If he now reaches out with his left arm, the fingers of the hand should just brush the bar. This will give an approximate distance to work to – final adjustment will come with experience and checking the high point of the jump in relation to the bar. It should, of course, come directly over the bar and half-way between the uprights.

There are many interpretations of the Straddle; no two jumpers perform it in precisely the same way. Basically, however, there are two accepted methods. In the first, the jumper leads over the bar with his head and shoulders draping himself around it. This method generally follows a bent free leg swing at take-off and many jumpers may have to be content with this interpretation because they are unable to utilize a straight swing of the non-jumping leg.

The second method with its numerous minor variations of execution, is used by the majority of world-class jumpers today. Here the jumper employs a high straight swing of the free leg and lies more along the bar as he crosses it. He then rolls away from the bar with his thighs open, landing on his side and back. The arms should be tucked into the sides, elbows bent, at bar level, coming away only to assist in cushioning the landing.

Recommended Form

1. Your jumping foot should be planted well in front of your body and your free (non-jumping) leg should begin to swing from your hip. At first it will be bent, but should very quickly straighten once the danger of it striking the ground is over.

2. Ideally you should have both your arms behind your body before the completion of the last stride. As the free leg begins its swing from the hip both your arms should be swung up in order to gain maximum possible momentum at take-off. However, many jumpers will not be able to co-ordinate the swing of both arms and will have to be content with swinging the inside arm and hunching the shoulder to balance the swing of the free (outside) leg.

3. As your jumping foot breaks contact with the ground, the free leg should be at its maximum possible height. You now rise to the bar rolling on to your stomach over the lath. Both your arms should now be tucked into your sides with the elbows bent close to your hips. Your hips should be high with your legs down on either side of the bar bent at the knee.

4. As you roll away from the bar the jumping leg, which is bent at the knee and below bar level on the take-off side, becomes a problem. It is best not to clear it from the lath by straightening it but rather to open out at the crutch with the knee remaining bent. In this way the leg will be cleared easily and in a relaxed manner.

5. The landing should be completed on the side and back – with a roll across your shoulders. Make certain that the pit is well dug and preferably have one that is built up some 2 ft

77

above ground level. The possibility of a bad landing can ruin the prospects of good form over the bar.

Training

During this period the young high jumper must carry out work for basic fitness; mobility exercises, weight training for strength and work on technique at the pit. The following are suggested activities for the athlete during this period:

1. Fartlek

Once a week do a 3–5 mile session of fartlek. Including uphill stretches now and again and vary the fast sections from 60 m to 200 m. It is preferable to do this work on soft ground rather than on the road.

2. Weight Training (3 days per week).

This is a necessary addition to your training in order to develop the strength to obtain an effective take-off. A typical schedule might include:

(a) *High Pull-ups.* 3 × 6. Warm-up.
(b) *Clean and Jerk.* 3 × 4. Leg drive and agility.
(c) *Abdominal Curl.* 2 × 10. 10 lb disc. Abdominal strength.
(d) *Toe Pushing.* 2 × 20. 80 lb. Toes resting on a 3 in. block. Extending the ankles and lowering the heels to the ground again.
(e) *Squat Jumps.* 3 × 6. Vary the angle at the knees from a position where the thighs are parallel to the ground to a $\frac{1}{4}$ squat position.
(f) *Two-hand Snatch.* 3 × 4. This is for agility and leg strength. It is a highly skilled exercise and it is suggested you start

with a light weight and attempt to learn the skill of the lift.
(g) *Military Press*. 3 × 6. Arms and shoulders.

Except where the poundages are shown you should start with a weight you can handle fairly comfortably for the set number of repetitions. The last repetition should be difficult and you should only just be able to complete the movement. This is the one that does you most good. As you improve so the poundage you handle should be increased. The schedule is only a suggestion and there will be many other schedules which will be equally as good. If possible seek the help of an expert to assist you in the early stages.

3. Jumping (2 days per week).

Jumping for technique should be done off a short approach at this stage. Vary the approach run from three to five strides and work on backward lean, free leg swing, single or double action and technique over the bar. The landing area should be built up or extremely well dug. Work can be done indoors by roping together twelve or sixteen inner tubes from motor-car tyres and placing rubber mats on top. This provides an area soft enough to allow a comfortable landing on the back for straddle jumpers.

4. Ballet Exercises

Many high jumpers carry out range of movement work with the ballet dancers. Since the jumper requires both mobility and strength this can be an extremely valuable addition to his winter training.

APRIL–MAY

During this period competition commences and therefore training begins to ease off slightly during May.

1. Interval Running (one day per week)

This should consist of a thorough warm-up including suppling exercises followed by a series of 60 m dashes from blocks with the sprinters.

2. Weight Training (two days per week).

Weight training should be continued but cut to two days per week. However, by the end of April it might be cut to one day per week with some isometric work substituted on the second of the two days.

3. Jumping (two days per week)

Jumping for technique off a full run should be carried out during April and early May. Once competition begins in earnest it would be best to cut the jumping sessions down to one day per week.

A typical week's work during this period might go something like this:

Monday

1. Warm-up consisting of jogging and wind sprints covering about three and a half laps. This should be followed by suppling and mobilizing exercises such as high kicking, trunk circling and bending, trying to obtain extreme range of movement with each repetition and a selected number of hurdling exercises. Place the bar at 8 ft 6 in. plus and carry out a series of high kicks breaking contact with the ground and rising as high and as straight as possible. The warm-up of the high jumper is very important and should be carried out thoroughly.
2. Jumping off a full run concentrating on those aspects of technique which require most attention (30 min).
3. Warm-down consisting of two laps jogging followed by some light loosening exercises.

Tuesday

1. Warm-up (as before).
2. Starting mark, check mark and take-off spot should be marked out on grass. Practise the approach run and take-off at normal speed, working for lean back, free leg swing, double or single arm action and lift. Leap straight up swinging the free leg straight and high. Land on both feet. Repeat this exercise until tired, working on the important aspects of take-off and concentrating on one thing at a time.
3. Warm-down (as before).

Wednesday

1. Warm-up (as before).
2. Jumping practice off a full approach concentrating on those aspects of technique which require most attention.
3. Warm-down (as before).

Thursday

1. Warm-up (as before).
2. Low hurdling (20 min).
3. Warm-down (as before).

Friday

Rest.

Saturday

Competition.

Sunday

1. Warm-up (as before).
2. 8 × 60 m (from blocks) walk back recovery.
3. Warm-down (as before).

Weight training sessions should be fitted in on Sunday, Monday or Wednesday. It would be better to carry out isometric work on Wednesday if this being done instead of one session of weight training.

JUNE–AUGUST

Monday

1. Warm-up (as before).
2. Jumping off a full approach consisting of six to eight attempts at a height within 3 in. of the jumper's best performance. Concentrate on timing and technique at bar level unless something has gone wrong with the approach and take-off during the last competition.
3. Warm-down (as before).

(i)   (ii)   (iii)   (iv)   (v)   (vi)

THE STRADDLE

(i) The jumping foot (left) has been planted well in front of the hips and upper body. The jumper's heel has contacted the ground ahead of the ball of the foot and he shows a position of backward lean. Note that the position of the right arm is forward; this is correct if the orthodox single-arm action is to be employed at take-off. However, if the jumper wishes to perfect a double arm action to improve momentum, then the right arm should have been pulled back into line with the left arm. From this backward position both arms are swung up together with the free leg.

(ii) The free leg (right) is swinging forward and upward from the hip. Note that the leg, having started bent, is now straight. It should remain straight and be travelling at its greatest speed as it passes through the horizontal position. The jumper has attempted to get his right arm back to employ a double-arm action, but it is clear from the picture that it has come too late to be really effective. Both arms should have been in position behind the body before the last stride had been completed. However, both arms are now swinging up together with the free leg.

(iii) The free leg has continued its long straight swing up to bar level. The right arm has now bent to move across the bar. The left arm from now on must be kept in a controlled position to avoid hitting the bar during clearance.

(iv) The jumping (left) leg has snapped up into a flexed position and the head and shoulders are beginning to go across and down on the far side of the bar. Note the excellent position of the right leg.

(v) Note the drapped position of the body at bar level. The head and right leg are down on the far side of the bar and the knee of the left leg is down on the take-off side. The arms are tucked into the sides, elbows bent. The left leg will now be cleared by the jumper lifting the left knee (still bent) and opening out at the crutch. Any vigorous straightening or swinging back of the left leg is to be avoided as it will set up embarrassing reactions in other parts of the body.

(vi) The jumper has now completed the clearance and is rolling away into the pit to land on the side and back. The left leg straightens only after it has crossed the bar, some jumpers maintain a bent position at the knee until they land.

Tuesday

1. Warm-up (as before).
2. Approach and take-off on grass as described before.
3. Warm-down (as before).

Wednesday

1. Warm-up (as before).
2. Low hurdling and light sprinting.
3. Warm-down (as before).

Thursday

1. Warm-up (as before).
2. 8 × 60 m (from blocks) walk back recovery.
3. Warm-down (as before).

Friday

Rest.

Saturday

Competition.

Sunday

Rest.

The Fosbury Flop

The series of pictures of Cornelia Popescu show the obvious advantages of this style of jumping. The curving approach means that the jumper is leaning away from the bar when she plants the foot at the completion of the last stride. This in turn leads to a direct upward thrust at take-off, the body weight being directly over the jumping foot and not leaning in towards the bar. The upper parts of the body, head and shoulders, are nearest to the bar and clear first. The body is then arched as far as mobility will allow and the legs jack-knifed for landing. After take-off the Fosbury jumper has two simple skills to perform. Firstly, the shoulders must be turned squarely to the bar after the scissor like take-off and, secondly, the hips arched and lifted in order to clear the bar. Notice that Cornelia

Popescu only turns her shoulders after she has broken contact with the ground. The fact that this turn has to be initiated whilst in contact with the ground need not concern the athlete. The jumper must think entirely of upward thrust and using the free limbs to assist with vertical lift.

6. The Triple Jump

At the present time there are two basic approaches to this event – the Polish method, which relies upon speed and a comparatively low trajectory in the three phases, and the Russian method which depends upon strength and agility, incorporating more bounce and height, particularly in the hop (first phase). The two methods have been compared by taking a theoretical 59 ft jump of the future:

Russian method:	59 ft	22 ft 3¾ in.	17 ft 0½ in.	19 ft 8 in.
Polish method:	59 ft	20 ft 8 in.	17 ft 8 in.	20 ft 8 in.

In 1954 the author had the opportunity of talking with L. Scherbacov, the Russian world-record holder, in Berne; he stated that he had to hop high in the first phase because he lacked speed, 11·1–11·2 for the 100 metres. This was borne out by his subsequent performance in the European Championships. Clearly the best way will ultimately be found by blending speed and strength to such an extent that the athlete will be able to use to the best advantage a really fast run-up and still be able to jump high on each of the three phases. This has been achieved in the high jump and long jump already and it cannot be long before an athlete is found capable of handling such a technique in the triple jump.

There are three principal methods of learning this event and the athlete should generally utilize all three with a bias towards his personal preference.

1. Even Rhythm

This is probably the most effective method, expecially in the first instance. The athlete should produce a ta-ta-ta on each landing, a regular beat and a positive bounce on into each jump. The middle phase (step) should be very nearly as long as the other phases (hop and jump). He should ignore the total distance achieved; working off a short run of five to seven strides, he should aim to produce an easy, regular and controlled action. In time this will develop naturally into a basically sound technique on which he may build the extras which make the champion.

2. Low Hop, building up Height in the Step and Jump

Although a steady increase in height throughout the three phases is undoubtedly a sound approach to learning the event, this does not actually happen in competition. The centre of gravity is lifted slightly higher in the hop than in the jump and the step (middle phase) is invariably the lowest. The jump is often further because the centre of gravity travels further down on landing.

However, the beginner invariably tends to hop too high and lose control and buckle at the knee on landing; this leads to a short step to enable him to recover sufficiently to achieve a reasonable jump. Therefore, the idea of controlling the height of the hop (first phase) is a good one whilst the athlete is in the early stages of his career. He should be able to obtain height in the last two phases after controlling the hop.

3. Ratio of Distance

Some beginners may find it useful to work to a set ratio of distance between the three phases. This however, is probably the least profitable line to pursue, as the correct ratio should come as a result of sound technique; it can seldom be artificially enforced. The novice might well find that a simple and comparatively easy target would be a ratio of 10:7:10, which works out at:

40 ft	= 14 ft 9½ in.	10 ft 5 in.	14 ft 9½ in.
12·19 m	= 4·50 m	3·19 m	4·50 m

By the time the jumper reaches 49 ft, the ratio will have altered to perhaps 10:8:10, which works out at:

49 ft	= 17 ft 9 in.	13 ft 6in.	17 ft 9 in.
14·93 m	= 5·41 m	4·11 m	5·41 m

There are many well-known variations which are of interest to the sudent of the triple jump and coach but of little practical value to the athlete. However, here is a table of distances which gives the athlete a target in the step (middle phase) for each distance. Remember, though, the hop (first phase) and (jump) (last phase) will vary according to the type of triple jumper.

40 ft = 14 ft 9½ in. — 10 ft 5 in. — 14 ft 9½ in.
41 ft = 15 ft 2 in. — 10 ft 8 in. — 15 ft 2 in.
42 ft = 15 ft 6 in. — 11 ft 0 in. — 15 ft 6 in.
43 ft = 15 ft 8½ in. — 11 ft 7 in. — 15 ft 8½ in.
44 ft = 16 ft 1 in. — 11 ft 10 in. — 16 ft 1 in.
45 ft = 16 ft 5 in. — 12 ft 2 in. — 16 ft 5 in.
46 ft = 16 ft 9 in. — 12 ft 6 in. — 16 ft 9 in.
47 ft = 17 ft 0½ in. — 12 ft 11 in. — 17 ft 0½ in.
48 ft = 17 ft 4½ in. — 13 ft 3 in. — 17 ft 4½ in.
49 ft = 17 ft 9 in. — 13 ft 6 in. — 17 ft 9 in.
50 ft = 18 ft 0 in. — 14 ft 0 in. — 18 ft 0 in.
51 ft = 18 ft 3 in. — 14 ft 6 in. — 18 ft 3 in.
52 ft = 18 ft 6 in. — 15 ft 0 in. — 18 ft 6 in.
53 ft = 18 ft 8 in. — 15 ft 8 in. — 18 ft 8 in.
54 ft = 18 ft 10 in. — 16 ft 4 in. — 18 ft 10 in.

Brendan Foster (Great Britain) in this picture illustrates the relaxed power of one of the world's greatest 5000m runners. In the Commonwealth Games in Christchurch he finished 2nd to Jipcho (Kenya) in the magnificent time of 13.14.6.

4 × 100m Relay, Olympic Games, Munich 1972. Valeri Borzov (USSR) takes the last leg from Yuri Silov (USSR). Note that Borzov is running on the outside of the lane and Silov coming in on the inside with the baton held in his right hand. Borzov is concentrating entirely on getting away fast and will receive the baton with an upsweep into his left hand.

George Woods (USA) displaying good technique during the Olympic Games, Munich 1972. He was second with a putt of 21.17 behind Wladyslaw Komar (Poland) 21.18.

John Bicourt (Great Britain). This picture illustrates an economical water-jump clearance. The position of the legs indicates that he is not going to drive hard off the rail but rather conserve energy and drop a little short into the water.

Alan Lerwill (Great Britain) competing in the Olympic Games Long Jump in Munich 1972. Many long jumpers fail because of their inability to obtain height in the jump after a fast approach run. Here Alan shows how high a world class long jumper raises his centre of gravity during the flight.

No. 147 R. Stecher (East Germany) wins the 1972 Olympic Games 200m final from Raelene Boyle (Australia). All the leading runners maintain good form in a very close finish.

This sequence shows Mike Bull competing in the Pole Vault. Note the hang position behind the pole in Fig 2, rock back in Figs 4 and 5, and clearance Fig 8.

2

1

6

5

The Fosbury Flop demonstrated by Cornelia Popescu.

Alan Pascoe (Great Britain) shows excellent drive and body-dip over the high hurdles. Note the way the right shoulder is well forward combining with an 'out and down' action of the right arm. He was gold medallist in the 400m hurdles in the 1974 Commonwaelth Games.

Ann Wilson (Great Britain) leads Judy Vernon (Great Britain) in the 100m hurdles race. Both girls illustrate the degree of concentration and timing required in this event.

To sum up, the beginner will do well to work to an even rhythm, at the same time keeping the first phase low. As he becomes more adept, he should begin to consider ratio and find out what suits him best. Now, by building up his strength speed and technical ability, set about improving the middle phase of the sequence. Improvement in this event can be rapid if the jumper uses his brain as well as his body to the best advantage.

Technique: Approach

The run-up should be much the same as in the long jump but with greater emphasis on control. The tyro should start with a short run in order to learn the event; five to nine strides will be satisfactory. Later on the run should be extended to between seventeen and twenty-three strides with one check mark inserted at least eight strides from the board. There is not the same necessity to coast over the last few strides as in the long jump where the jumper rears back, at the board to gain height. The triple jumper will inevitably have a lower trajectory and can, therefore, afford to run on to the board with merely an erect trunk and a drop in tension. It is preferable to arrange the approach so that the strongest leg (take-off leg in the long jump) is used twice in the first two phases (hop and step). In time, by weight training and various forms of apparatus work to build up strength in the non-jumping leg, this inequality of leg strength may be ironed out.

First Phase (Hop)

The body moves faster over the take-off foot than in the long jump; the final drive is lower and finishes further behind the centre of gravity. This gives a greater tendency to forward rotation which must be counteracted by keeping the trunk erect and the head in line with the body at take-off. In other respects the take-off is the same as in the long jump—the lift of the knee of the non-jumping leg to gain momentum and give some backward rotation and the normal balancing action of the arms. The arms are used as balancers during the hop. Kreer. (U.S.S.R.) manages to bring them both back by the end of the hop so they may both be used as a double arm action to assist with momentum at the beginning of the step. However, the beginner is well advised to be content with bringing the opposite arm to the free leg through vigorously. The free leg is swung back in the air, which action in itself is a form of hitch-kick, so that on landing the leg is trailing and there is a split between the legs.

Second Phase (Step)

The first essential of a good step is an active landing from the hop. The free leg, which is trailing, should be brought through vigorously with knee bent and the opposite arm balancing. Meantime the landing and driving leg is swung back and down to the ground to obtain drive and bounce into the step. The jumper now lifts the knee of the free leg high and tilts the trunk slightly forward. At this stage he may swing both arms back to be used simultaneously at the take-off for the jump. He, should now wait for the ground to come to him, and as it does make an explosive landing to get the best out of himself in the final jump.

Third Phase (Jump)

As he lands from the step the non-jumping leg is trailing well behind the body, both arms are back ready to be swung through and the leg to be used in the final jump is poised, knee held high, ready to be swung powerfully back and down to the ground. The jumper now waits for the ground to come to him and as it does explodes into the final jump. The trailing leg swings through, both arms drive forward and upward as the jumping leg strokes the ground powerfully away. The final landing is made with the feet held as high as possible, the arms being used to assist the body over the fulcrum of the feet in the pit.

Building Up the Event

1. You should incorporate weight training, hopping, bounding, giant strides and general exercises of strength and mobility from the beginning of your training.

2. You can also do much useful work in the gymnasium during the winter months, such as bounding on and off boxes with a gradual increase in height, standing hop, step and jump practice and work off three and five strides. Also hop, hop and jump testing one leg against the other. Do a standing hop, hop and jump off the left leg six times and repeat off the right leg. Try this off three and five strides as you get more adept.

3. As soon as the weather and facilities permit, go outside and work on soft grass. This is always preferable to a cinder run-up at this stage of your training. M. Ralph (Great Britain) produced the following figure at the Loughborough Summer School in 1961:

Standing Triple Jump (off grass into the pit)

Hop	Step	Jump	Total Distance
7 ft 8 in.	9 ft 10 in.	11 ft 8 in.	29 ft 2 in.
7 ft 8 in.	10 ft 2 in.	12 ft 9 in.	30 ft 7 in.
7 ft 5 in.	10 ft 0 in.	13 ft 1 in.	30 ft 6 in.

The steady increase in distance is brought about as the speed increases from the stationary start.

4. Work entirely to an even ryhthm until the general pattern of the sequence has become second nature to you. Try to obtain as much bounce and lift as you can in the step and jump. You should not attempt a full-length run at this stage; if you do, your form will go to pieces and your step (middle phase) will once more be reduced to a mere recovery from the hop (first phase).

5. Do not attempt to split this event into parts and learn it phase by phase. It is a complete movement and the balance and co-ordination between each phase is the whole essence of the event.

6. Now use the pit with a seven-stride run trying to achieve a good split between the legs on each landing and gather for the final jump with a high knee pick-up in the step.

7. You should now try a nine-stride run with a 2 ft hurdle or worsted tape inserted in the middle of the step to encourage bounce and height. At the same time put a series of hurdles close together at 3 ft and hop consecutively over them. Now go back using the other leg; repeat until fatigued.

8. Take your run back to eleven strides and increase the height of the hurdle to 2 ft 6 in. You may now start to work on other points of technique after removing the hurdle: a controlled lowish hop with height and bounce in the step and jump, also correct balance and double arm action for the final jump.

9. Finally, to perfect this event, you must *do* it, and when you increase to a full run keep it under control. Don't attempt too much speed all at once otherwise you will find yourself back where you started with a short recovery in the step.

Training

The winter training of a triple jumper is very similar to that of the long jumper. In fact, expecially with the young athlete, these two events can dovetail together very easily. The following are some activities the triple jumper may carry out during the winter months:

1. Fartlek

Once or twice a week do a 3–5 mile session of fartlek. Include an uphill stretch of about 200 m and vary the speed work over 60–200 m. It is preferable to do this work over soft ground; work on the roads is a poor but sometimes necessary substitute.

2. Weight Training

This is a necessary adjunct to your training in order to build up the required strength, not only in the legs but also in the rest of the body. The triple jumper is particularly prone to back, knee and ankle injuries if he is not strong in relation to his bodyweight. The schedule can be very similar to the one laid down for the long jumper. However, step-ups should be added to the schedule. Fred Alsop (Great Britain) has used steps-ups on to a 14 in.–16 in. bench with a suitably padded bar placed across the shoulders with weight up to 250 lb. This height of bench produces a right angle at the knee when the stepping foot is on the box and this is desirable. This exercise will strengthen thigh and calf muscles, also knee and ankle joints.

Step-ups: 3 × 10 repetitions leading with one leg for the first half-set of ten and the other leg of the second half-set, twenty repetitions in all. Take a minute's rest and then repeat. The novice should start with a weight which he can handle fairly comfortably for the complete exercise. As he improves, so the weight should be increased and the number of repetitions decreased.

3. Gymnasium

Work in the gymnasium may be carried out on one or two nights a week as described in 'Building Up the Event', Paragraph 2.

4. Jumping

Jumping for form off a short run may be done outside whenever conditions permit. At this stage three to seven strides would be a suitable distance, concentrating all the time on points of technique. This may be varied by doing hop, hop, jumps off first one leg then the other, also the use of a weighted jacket can be very beneficial during these practices.

5. Towards the end of February some interval running should be included once per week 8×150 m (fast stride) rest of lap jog to recover.

APRIL–MAY

During this period competition commences, therefore training should begin to ease off a bit towards the end of May.

1. Interval Running (two days per week)

Interval running is now substituted for the fartlek sessions. The triple jumper should carry out much the same type of work as the long jumper in this respect:

1st day

6×150 m (full effort) 4 min recovery.

2nd day

(a) 10 × 60 m (full effort) from blocks walk back recovery.
(b) Low hurdling over three hurdles (15 min).

2. Weight Training

Weight training should be continued on two days per week during April but might be cut to one day per week during May, with isometric work being done on the second day. However, many triple jumpers would prefer to keep two days' weight training going throughout this period. If you wish to substitute isometric work you are advised to consult a physical education specialist.

3. Jumping (two days per week)

Jumping off a short run may be followed by a few jumps off a full approach. Since this will be done on the track with a cinder approach the heels should be protected. It is easy to set up an injury early in the season by coming straight out on to the track and jumping at full effort from a full approach without adequate protection. Either sponge rubber pads should be placed inside the heels of the shoes or heel cups should be worn. This also applies to the long jumper at this stage.

A typical week's work at this period might go something like this:

Monday

(a) Warm-up, consisting of jogging followed by a series of fast strides down the straight covering about 80 m. This should be followed by mobilizing and suppling exercises and a series of giant strides obtaining as much bound and lift as possible. The whole warm-up should take about 25–30 min.
(b) Jumping off a short run followed by three jumps off a full approach at maximum effort. Concentrate throughout on

95

good form or a fault that may have become apparent during Saturday's competition.

(c) Warm-down.

(d) Weight training (this may be carried out later in the day.)

Tuesday

(a) Warm-up (as before).

(b) 6 × 150 m (full effort) 4 min recovery.

(c) Warm-down (as before).

Wednesday

(a) Warm-up (as before).

(b) Jumping off a short approach, preferably on grass. Concentrate on lift and bounce.

(c) Warm-down.

(d) Weight training or isometric work (this may be done later in the day).

Thursday

(a) Warm-up (as before)

(b) 10 × 60 m (full effort from blocks) walk back recovery.

(c) Low hurdling over three hurdles (15 min).

(d) Warm-down.

Friday

Rest.

Saturday

Competition.

Sunday

Light sprinting or weight training on this day instead of Wednesday.

During this period your training should ease off considerably and only a very little, if any, jumping should be included during August.

Monday

(a) Warm-up (as before).
(b) Either a little jumping off a short run to correct faults or sprint starting practice.
(c) Warm-down.

Tuesday

(a) Warm-up (as before).
(b) 8 × 60 m (full effort) walk back recovery.
(c) Warm-down.
(d) Weight training or isometric work (this may be done later in the day.)

Wednesday

(a) Warm-up (as before).
(b) Check and practise full approach run with a light jump. some further jumping may be done off a full run if you feel it to be necessary but not as a general rule.
(c) Warm-down.

Thursday

(a) Warm-up (as before).
(b) Low hurdling with the hurdles placed so you may take four or eight strides between, thus leading with the left leg and right legs alternately.
(c) Warm-down.

G

Friday

Rest.

Saturday

Competition.

Sunday

Light sprinting and weight training or isometric work.

JUMP   STEP   HOP

Reading from right to left this illustration shows the complete sequence of the triple jump. The non-jumping leg is brought up vigorously at take-off and the high position of the knee is held fractionally after leaving the board. The leg is now swung back staight in a modified hitch-kick action; this has produced some backward displacement of the trunk and helped to maintain balance in the air. In the middle part of the hop, the arms are used as balancers. On landing, the non-jumping leg is now trailing and there is a split between the thighs; the trailing leg can now come through vigorously to assist with momentum and lift in the step.

The landing from the hop must be an active one and at the same time the trailing leg and opposite arm must be brought through vigorously as shown in the diagrams of the step phase. In the middle of the step, the knee of the forward leg maintains its high position and the trunk tilts forward. The jumper now waits for the ground to come to him and when it does, explodes into the final jump. Note the position shown on landing with the trailing leg well back ready to be brought through rapidly to assist in gaining momentum.

In this series the jumper is employing an orthodox single arm action during the take-off for the jump. However, many jumpers would have brought both arms back prior to take-off for the final phase and would swing them both up with the non-jumping leg. The novice will in all probability find it better to use the ordinary sail technique in the final jump. These pictures show a modified hang style which is recommended for the more accomplished triple jumper.

7. The Long Jump

The essence of good long jumping lies in the ability to obtain a high jump at the end of a fast approach. The mistake often made in the past has been to emphasize sprinting speed to the exclusion of the vital factor of spring. The three most important factors in this event are: (a) speed at the take-off, (b) upward spring at the board, (c) a good landing with the feet well up and forward in relation to the centre of gravity of the body as the heels cut the sand. The most difficult of these three is getting height off the board, and most of the long jumper's training should be devoted to perfecting this part of the event. There is little point in discussing the ideal angle of take-off because no athlete jumps high enough after a full-speed approach. The aim should always to be obtain more height without loss of speed by checking at the board.

The Approach Run

The total distance will vary between 90 ft and 130 ft and in some extreme cases a run of 140 ft may be used. This means the jumper will be taking between seventeen and twenty-three strides in the run-up. The odd number is generally used so he may hit the check mark or marks and take-off board all with the same foot. However, many jumpers walk, trot or run on to the starting mark; in this case consistency of the early strides becomes very important. The novice would be well advised to start his run with the feet together, toeing his starting mark, and to step off with the foot with which he wishes to hit his check marks and the board.

The Take-off

The jumper should have reached maximum possible speed some distance from the board. During the last four strides he will have to make the necessary adjustments to his body carriage to enable him to obtain an effective spring from the board This will mean a drop in tension, a more erect position of the trunk and a lowering of the hips. The take-off foot is planted in front of the bodyweight and slightly across towards the centre line. This will enable him to apply his force directly underneath the centre of gravity of the body.

The exact length of each of the last three strides is rather an individual matter. In most cases the penultimate stride is lengthened and the last stride shortened in relation to it. However, more height may be obtained by a marked lowering of the hips on the penultimate stride, which will have the effect of shortening this stride. This in turn will mean that the take-off foot will be planted further in front of the centre of gravity of the body. which will allow the jumper to apply force for a greater length of time. However, only a jumper with a great deal of leg strength and very good co-ordination would be able to perfect this technique. Nevertheless, it is something to be aimed at in the course of time, always provided, of course, that forward speed is not lost by too violent a check at the board.

As the jumper comes over his take-off foot, the opposite leg, knee bent, is being swung forward and upward rapidly to gain momentum, also the opposite arm, For the left-footed jumper this will mean the left arm and right leg. While these limbs are being used to gain momentum, an equal and opposite force is going down through the jumping leg in reaction.

Style in the air

Although the jumper may take off with backward rotation, forward rotation or no rotation at all, generally speaking in an effective jump he will leave the board with forward rotation. He will tend to rotate forward about an axis which passes transversely through his hips. In order to counteract this forward rotation, either the hitch-kick or hang techniques may be used. However, there is nothing one can do, once having broken contact with the ground, to gain momentum in the air. All each of these styles can do is put the jumper in a good landing position and, therefore gain perhaps 6 in. to 8 in. at the end of the jump.

The Hang

After take-off, the jumper straightens the non-jumping leg, which had been brought up to hip level as he left the board, and swings it back and down to join the jumping leg which is left behind. His body is now extended in the air, legs trailing. The arms work together, first swinging back, then round, over and forwards. The legs are now flexed and brought through bent, the feet being held up and forwards for the landing.

The Hitch-kick

The jumper takes off in the normal way, and as he rises to the high point of the jump the non-jumping leg is straightened and swung back and down. In the meantime, the take-off leg is brought through bent, then extended forwards ready for the landing. The non-jumping leg, having folded up behind the thigh, is now swept through bent to join the take-off leg which is already forward and the feet cut the sand together.

The Landing

A good landing position is one where the upper body is as erect as possible, the legs outstretched and well up and forward as the heels cut the sand. It is best if the arms are thrown back immediately prior to landing. Once the feet have cut the sand the arms should be thrown forward and upward to, assist the body over the fulcrum of the feet.

Training

OCTOBER–MARCH

During the winter months a strenuous building-up programme should be undertaken; this should include work for basic fitness and strength as well as jumping for height off a short run. The following are suggested activities for the young long jumper during this period:

1. Fartlek

Once or twice a week do a 3–5 mile session of fartlek. Include an uphill stretch of about 200 m and vary the speed work over 60–200 m. It is preferable to do this work over soft ground; work on the roads is a poor but sometimes necessary substitute.

2. Weight Training (three days per week)

This is a necessary adjunct to your training in order to build up the necessary strength, not only in the legs but also abdomen and other parts of the body, to enable you to obtain height after a fast approach run.

A typical schedule would include:

(a) High pull-ups. 3 × 6. Warm-up.

(b) Clean and jerk. 3 × 4. Leg drive and agility.

(c) Abdominal curl. 2 × 10. 10 lb disc. Abdominal strength.

(d) Squat jumps. 3 × 6. Leg strength. Vary depth of squat on each repetition. But don't go too low—thighs parallel to the ground only.

(e) Two-hand snatch. 3 × 4. Again for agility and leg strength. This is a highly skilled exercise and it is suggested that you start with a light weight and attempt to learn the skill of this lift. The practice will be of great benefit to you. In time you will become skilled and be able to handle a reasonable weight.

(f) Straddle lift, 3 × 6. Leg strength. Here you handle a heavy load with safety.

Remember there are many weight-training schedules that will be equally as good as this one—the above is only a suggestion. If you are a novice at weight training, you must obtain the help and advice of an expert before embarking on a schedule similar to the above.

3. Jumping (two days per week)

Although it is important to learn either the hitch-kick or hang techniques during the winter, if you have not already done so, it is far more important to practise jumping for height off a short run. The practise should be off five strides only. Lowering the hips slightly over the last three strides, drive up, using the momentum from the bent free leg and the opposite arm to assist. Hold the high position of the knee of the free leg off the board, then either go into a hang or hitch-kick or just hold the feet well up for landing. Sit down in the pit as you will not have the speed to come over the fulcrum of your feet.

104

In early spring (March–April), begin to increase the length and speed of your run-up, still trying to obtain height off the board. You will find that you gradually improve. Do not be discouraged at your first attempts at a full run and take-off; to begin with it is unlikely that you will get much carry-over from the winter practice until you have had several sessions at the pit.

4. Interval Running

Interval running should be included from the end of February 8 × 150 m (fast stride) rest of lap jog to recover.

APRIL–MAY

During this period competition commences and, therefore, training begins to ease off slightly during May.

1. Interval Running (two days per week)

Interval running is now substituted for the fartlek sessions. The following schedule is suggested for long jumpers:

1st day
6 × 50 m (full effort) 4 min recovery.

2nd Day
10 × 60 m (full effort from blocks) walk back recovery.

Weight Training (two days per week)

Weight training should be continued on two days per week during April but might be cut to one day per week during May with isometric work being done on the second day. However, many jumpers would prefer to keep two day weight training going throughout this period. If you wish to substitute isometric work you are advised to consult a physical education specialist.

3. Jumping (two days per week)

Jumping off a short run followed by a few jumps from a full approach at speed. Your technique in the air and landing should be perfected at this time.

A typical weeks work during this period might go something like this:

Monday

(a) Warm-up, consisting of jogging followed by a series of strides down the straight covering about 80 m. These should be at a steady pace to begin with, followed by several fast stretches at full speed. Mobilizing and suppling exercises should follow, the whole warm-up taking about 25 min.

(b) Jumping off a short run, concentrating on technique in the air and the landing. Hold your feet well up and sit down in in the pit after your feet have cut the sand. You will not have sufficient speed to complete the landing off such a short run. Finish with three full-effort jumps off a long approach, trying to obtain as much height as possible off the board.

(c) Weight training.

Tuesday

(a) Warm-up (as before).

(b) 6 × 150 m (full effort) 4 min recovery. Work for even stride length and relaxation in your running.

(c) Warm-down.

Wednesday

(a) Warm-up (as before).

(b) Jumping off a short approach for height.
(c) Weight training.

Thurdsay

(a) Warm-up (as before).
(b) 10 × 60 m (full effort from blocks) walk back recovery.
(c) Warm-down.

Friday

Rest.

Saturday

Competition.

Sunday

Light sprinting and thorough mobilizing and suppling work.

JUNE–AUGUST

During this period your training should ease off considerably and only a very little, if any, jumping should be included during August.

Monday

(a) Warm-up (as before).
(b) Either a little jumping off a short run to correct faults or sprint starts with the sprinters.
(c) Warm-down.

Tuesday

(a) Warm-up (as before).
(b) 8 × 60 m (full effort) walk back recovery.
(c) Warm-down.

(vi)   (v)   (iv)   (iii)   (ii)   (i)

THE HANG

These pictures show the complete sequence of the Hang Style reading from right to left.

(i) The jumping leg is now completing its drive and the body has moved in front of the take-off foot. The right leg and left arm have been brought through correctly to assist in gaining momentum at this most important stage of the jump.

(ii) The jumper has now left the board and is correctly holding the take-off position with the right knee in line with the hips. The hang action should be delayed slightly off the board otherwise the jumper is tempted to pull the right leg (non-jumping leg) back prematurely, thus losing valuable momentum at take off.

(iii) The arms have been swept down, round and back, working together. The right leg has straightened and bent swung back in a hitch-kick action and the whole body extended in order to slow down the angular velocity. The hang incorporates a hitch-kick action with the non-jumping leg, and this is one of the advantages of this technique.

(iv) The arms are now sweeping down and forward and the legs are being brought through bent for the landing. Both legs being brought through together tends to pull the trunk down in reaction. Hence it is of the utmost importance to lessen the moment of inertia by keeping them bent during this stage of the jump.

(v) The arms are now sweeping back and the legs have completed their forward movement and have been straightened in preparation for the landing. The trunk has been dragged down as the legs came through.

(vi) The legs have dropped a little before cutting the sand and the trunk has come slightly more upright in reaction. Now the feet are about to enter the pit, the arms will now be swept forward to assist the jumper over his heels.

(d) Weight training. This may be done later in the day or isometric work substituted.

Wednesday

(a) Warm-up (as before).
(b) Check and practise full approach run and take-off with a light jump. Some further jumping off a full run may be done if you feel it to be necessary but not as a general rule.

Thurdsay

(a) Warm-up (as before).
(b) Low hurdling with three hurdles out for even striding. Place the hurdles about 17 m apart or a suitable distance for a seven-stride rhythm between.
(c) Warm-down.

Friday

Rest.

Saturday

Competition.

Sunday

Weight training or isometric work.

(i) The jumping leg has now completed its drive and the body has moved in front of the take-off foot. The right arm and left leg have been brought through correctly to assist in gaining momentum.

(ii) The left leg has now straightened and begun its backward swing and the right leg (take-off leg) is being brought through bent. The arms are counter-balancing the legs, swinging back, round and over, the left arm leading the right.

(iii) The left leg has almost completed its backward swing and the right leg has been drawn through bent and close to its axis of movement. This is the vital part of the hitch-kick, the backward movement made with a straight leg and the forward movement with a bent leg. The body is now in an extended position which, in itself, slows down the forward rotation which is generally present after a good take-off.

(iv) The right leg is now extended for the landing and the left leg is being brought through bent to join it. The arms continue their forward movement, the right arm now beginning to catch up the left arm.

(v) Both legs are now up and forward prior to cutting the sand and the arms are moving down and back together.

(vi) The heels have now entered the sand and the arms will be brought forward to assist the jumper over the fulcrum of his feet. A conscious effort should be made to hold the feet and legs up prior to landing.

8. The Pole Vault

The introduction of the Bantex glass fibre pole has brought modern pole vaulting technique within the reach of junior vaulters and schools. These poles are graded to the individual and the schoolboy can learn to bend the pole without difficulty and with complete safety. However, an adequate foam-filled, built-in landing area must also be provided. Ideally this would be 3 ft high, 16 ft 4 in. wide and 16 ft 4 in. in length. Extensions on each side of the vaulting box should be the same height as the landing area and extended 3 ft towards the runway and approximately 4 ft to 6 ft wide.

For seniors, poles are again graded to the individual and a vaulter weighing 160 lb should, in competition and vaulting for height, use a pole tested to support 160 lb at the height of of his grip. However, vaulters will use lighter poles in training to practise techniques off a short approach.

Grip and Carry

The height of grip is measured from the top of the right hand to the bottom of the pole, less 8 in. to account for the end of the pole which enters the box. This is known as the effective grip on the pole. Every pole bends more easily in one direction and to find this the vaulter should roll the pole through his fingers with the end resting on the ground. The pole will always come to rest in the same position and this indicates the preference of bend. In order to determine the exact carry position, the vaulter should place the pole in the box adopting the correct plant position with the point of bend facing NNW for the right-handed vaulter. Now gripping the pole firmly he lowers it to his side in the carry position. The pole rotates in a clockwise direction and adhesive tape can now be placed on the uppermost side of the pole whilst in the correct carry position. This will now serve as a marker for the vaulter as he takes up his position at the end of the runway in readiness to begin the approach run.

Most vaulters grip the pole with the hands some two feet apart. The lower hand can either grip the pole tightly with an overgrasp or it can merely rest on the thumb with the other fingers wrapped loosely over the top of the shaft. A firm grip is normally adopted with the upper hand (right hand) with black insulating tape and adhesive sprays to ensure the hand does not slip during the vault. No more than two thicknesses of tape may be used and this rule is strictly enforced at major meetings.

The Approach

The beginner, having learnt to bend a floppy pole and clear a height, will progress to an approach run of 7 to 9 strides and then increase it to 11 strides.

Sprinting with the pole is a very necessary practice for all vaulters. The pole should be pointing straight down the runway with the point in line with the left shoulder. It is speed over the last 3 strides into and through the plant which will enable the vaulter to bend a stiff pole with good results. 60 m dashes with the pole should be a normal part of every training session on the track.

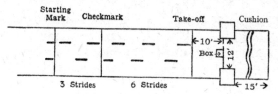

The above is a simple plan of a nine-stride approach suitable for the average schoolboy. The distance from take-off spot to stop board is put down as 10 ft. This will vary slightly of course from athlete to athlete. Over such a short distance as nine strides the checkmark may in time be found unnecessary. But generally speaking it should be adhered to.

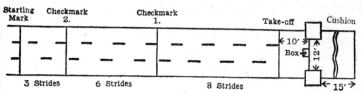

This shows a seventeen-stride approach for the more accomplished vaulter. However, as has been stated in the text, many vaulters would use a run-up of nineteen to twenty-three strides In some cases they prefer to walk and run on to a first checkmark which might be seventeen or nineteen strides from the take-off spot. The vaulter must take into account the tiring and very often protracted nature of his event. Therefore, when deciding on the total length of run, it is a wise precaution to ensure that he is not using up energy wastefully by employing an approach run which is too long for his capabilities.

The Plant and Take-off

These are the two most important phases of the vault; 75% of all the faults in the air can be traced back to poor plant which, in turn, can be attributed to other technical faults during the approach and last three strides.

The pole plant is commenced three strides from the take-off. The pole is lowered and thrust forward and downward into the box hitting the back of the box a fraction of a second before the left foot lands at the end of the last stride. At the same time it is thrust up and over the head (Fig 2). This picture illustrates a good position immediately after take-off with the pole beginning to bend as the vaulter drives straight forward.

The plant must be made early; a late plant is one of the worst faults a vaulter can make. It is a very common fault of the novice because co-ordination must be perfect in order to achieve a smooth movement without loss of momentum. The arms should work close to the body as the pole goes forward. Some vaulters employ a slight shift of the left (lower) hand up the pole while others maintain the same position as they had in the carry. Adhesive tape and venice turpentine also help to consolidate the position of the power hand at this stage. At take-off the left foot should be directly under or very slightly ahead of the upper hand (Fig 2). The left arm is bent at the elbow and should hold the body away from the pole by maintaining a fixed position. Mike Bull illustrates this point extremely well.

The Rock Back

After take-off the vaulter hangs momentarily behind the pole (Fig 3). From this position the rock back begins; this brings the vaulter into a position which will ensure a good vertical lift when the pole recoils. A good rock back will be obtained in the following way:

The right arm remains straight while the left arm, flexed at the elbow, holds the body away from the pole. The axis of rotation should be about the shoulders as the hips and legs go up towards the top of the pole (Fig 4). Note that the hips in Fig 5 are well above the shoulders and the feet right at the top of the pole. If the hip do not get high enough the vaulter will be thrown at and into the bar, not up and over it for a clearance.

Pull and Turn

The vaulter should stay on his back and wait for as long as possible before beginning the pull and turn. A common fault, as the bar gets towards the vaulter's maximum height, is to begin the turn too soon. Mike Bull shows a good position in Fig 6 with the legs right up the pole and the body vertical The pull, turn and clearance should be fast and late with the final push going straight down the pole (Fig 7).

Clearance

The left hand breaks contact with the pole first and is lifted up and away from the bar. The right arm continues to push down the pole until it is fully extended. The legs must not drop; all parts of the body must continue to move upwards until the right hand has completed its final thrust. The vaulter should think of a position with the head down, thumbs in and elbows out as the push takes place. This will hollow the chest and assist with the clearance. After breaking contact with the ground through the pole, further hip height can be obtained by piking over the bar. The landing is now made on the back providing the landing area is adequate.

Training Schedules

OCTOBER–MARCH

During this period the vaulter must work to improve his basic skill in the vault, agility, speed and strength. The following are suggested activities for the vaulter during the winter months:

Skill Practice

At least two sessions per week should be spent vaulting in order to improve various points of technique. While the weather is good it is best to take advantage of it and get out to the track whenever possible.

Work in the Gymnasium

One or two nights can be spent in the gymnasium doing agilities and apparatus gymnastics. The vaulter can finish off this period with a session of circuit training designed for the pole vaulter. This might include rope climbing and strong abdominal work.

Weight Training

Weight training should be carried out on three days per week with one days rest between sessions. The vaulter must be strong; strength is an absolute necessity for ultimate success in this event .The following exercises might be included in the schedule:

1. High pull-ups.
2. Bicep curls.
3. Tricep curls.
4. Bench presses.
5. Abdominals.
6. Cleans and jerks.

The beginner should work With comparatively light weights, carrying out a lot of repetitions, perhaps two sets of two repetitions, The more experienced athlete will use heavier weights with fewer repetitions, perhaps three sets of five repetitons.

However, it is best for the novice to seek the help of a specialist in physical education who is on the spot to assess his requirements.

Fartlek or Interval Running

One session of fartlek or interval running on the track is advised for general fitness. The pole vaulter often tends to get so bogged down with skill and strength work that he neglects this important aspect of his training.

A typical winter training schedule might go something like this:

Monday
1. Warm-up with jogging, striding and short sprints followed by exercises for mobility, agility and strength (15 min).
2. Weight training (30 min).
3. Warm-down (10 min easy running and light exercises).

Tuesday
1. Warm-up (as before).
2. Vaulting for form at the pit. This might involve twenty to twenty-five vaults for form, including some at a height just above the athlete's capabilities. The vaulter must get used to the timing of the vault at extreme heights in training if he wishes to be successful in competition.
3. Warm-down (as before).

Wednesday : Gymnasium
1. Warm-up.
2. Agility work and apparatus gymnastics (30 min).
3. Weight training (30 min).
4. Warm-down (light exercises).

Thursday

1. Warm-down (as before).
2. Vaulting for form (45 min).
3. Sprint starts (10 min).
4. Warm-down (10 min easy running and light exercises).

Friday

1. Fartlek or interval running.
2. Weight training.
3. Warm-down (as before).

Saturday

Either vaulting at the pit or another session in the gymnasium as done on wednesday.

Sunday

Rest.

APRIL–MAY

Monday

1. Warm-up (as before).
2. Vaulting for form until tired.
3. Weight training.
4. Warm-down.

Tuesday

1. Warm-up (as before).
2. 10 × 60 m (full effort) walk back recovery.
3. Agility exercises and rope climbing, etc.
4. Warm-down (as before).

Wednesday

1. Warm-up (as before).
2. Vaulting for form: a dozen vaults should be enough but don't be afraid to take more if necessary. In this early part of the sesson it is better for the novice to do too much vaulting than too little; the technique must be thoroughly grooved in.
3. Warm-down (as before).

Thursday: Gymnasium

Apparatus gymnastics and agility work.

Friday

Rest.

Saturday

Competition or pole-vault trial.

Sunday

Rest or light fartlek.

JUNE–AUGUST

Monday

1. Warm-up (as before).
2. About twenty vaults for form working on any faults shown during Saturday's competition.
3. Warm-down (as before).

Tuesday

1. Warm-up (as before).
2. 10 × 60 m (full effort) walk back recovery.

3. Light weight training or isometric work.
4. Warm-down (as before).

Wednesday
1. Warm-up (as before).
2. A dozen vaults for form.
3. Low hurdling (10 min).
4. Warm-down (as before).

Thursday
Light exercise, agility work and sprinting.

Friday
Rest.

Saturday
Competition.

Sunday
Rest.

The sequence of photographs taken by Tissot van Patot shows Mike Bull (Gt. Britain) vaulting five metres in the European Championships, Athens 1969.

(i) He is in an upright position two strides out from the take-off shown in Fig 2. The plant is now beginning, the pole being lowered and thrust forward towards the box. Thus the right arm and right leg go forward together, a movement which must be practised and perfected because it is contrary to normal body mechanics. An early plant is the key to a good vault and this is the aspect of vaulting which the novice must spend most of his time perfecting.

(ii) This shows the take-off with the right arm extended but slightly flexed and the left foot under and slightly ahead of the upper hand. The right knee is driving forward in a good position and the left arm is firmly bent holding him away from the pole This fixed position of the left arm keeps the vaulter behind the pole during this vital stage of the vault.

(iii) He has passed through the hang position, staying behind the pole as he attempts to swing momentarily forward rather than upward. If this stage of the vault is hurried it will have disastrous results later on.

(iv) Both legs are going up towards the top of the pole bent at the knees. The hips have risen above the shoulders and will be going on up. The pole having reached maximum bend is now beginning to recoil with the mass of Mike Bull's body weight behind it.

(v) As the pole straightens so do the vaulter's legs and he reaches upwards towards the top of the pole with his feet. He attempts to lie on his back and wait as the hips continue to rise above the shoulders.

(vi-viii) The pole has now completely extended and the vaulter is moving vertically upwards. From this position the sequence of pull, turn and push commences very rapidly and the completion of the vault is well illustrated in Figs 7-8. While still in contact with the pole (Fig 7) the vaulter must attempt to keep all parts of the body moving upwards. Only on leaving the pole (Fig 8) should he 'pike' his body to attempt to gain hip height in the clearance.

9. Putting the Shot

Since Parry O'Brien (U.S.A.) adopted a starting position facing to the rear of the circle and incorporating a glide across the circle with the head and shoulders facing squarely back, the world record has steadily improved and the general standard of shot putting throughout the athletic nations of the world has rocketed upwards. A lot of this must be attributed to the fact that most champions have adopted Parry O'Brien's method, or some modification of the same general pattern. However, another and very obvious reason for the general improvement is the importance all modern throwers attach to muscular strength. Not only are shot putters today fast, big men but but they are also stronger physically than their predecessors. The modern champion is not only a big man but he is usually a reasonable sprinter over short distances, exceptionally strong in relation to his bodyweight, agile and well co-ordinated.

Technique: Holding the Shot

An easy and quick method for the novice to obtain the correct hold is to place the shot in the palm of the hand, fingers spread. Now rock the ball up so it rests on the first joints at the base of the fingers. The athlete will now see that the three middle fingers are comfortably spread behind the shot and the thumb and little finger on either side for balance. It should lie slightly towards the index finger and thumb, the stronger side of the hand.

It should now be placed into the neck, resting on the collar bone and underneath the jaw, the heel of the hand below the shot, palm of the hand up and slightly facing towards the left. As the thrower becomes more experienced and his technique improves, he will be able to hold the shot higher up on the fingers and a little further out of the palm of the hand. This depends on his ability to accelerate the shot with the legs and body before the arm, wrist and fingers play their part in the final delivery.

The Starting Position

The technique referred to from now on will be the O'Brien style as performed by a right-handed thrower.

The athlete should adopt a standing position at the rear of the circle, his back to the general line of direction and trunk erect. The toes of the right foot should be up against the circle and pointing directly to the rear. The toes of the left foot should tap the ground about 18 in. towards the front of the circle with the leg relaxed. The left arm should be raised above the head, the palm of the hand facing out and away from the body towards the rear. The right hand holds the shot as previously described: into the neck resting on the collar bone and underneath the jaw.

The head should be upright, with the eyes focused about 10–15 ft behind the circle on a marker previously positioned for this purpose. Throughout the preliminary stance, glide and start of the delivery action at the front of the circle, the eyes should be kept fixed on this point.

The Glide or Shift

The faster the missile leaves the hand, the further it is going to go. The object of the glide is therefore:

(a) To generate as much forward speed as possible across the circle.

(b) To land with the body in a position, at the front of the circle from which the athlete can put the shot effectively whilst still on the move.

If an effective glide is added to a sound putting position, the athlete can expect an improvement of approximately one-seventh of the distance of a good standing put. However, if the novice attempts to achieve too much speed in the glide, he may jeopardize his chance of obtaining a good throwing position at the end of the movement. The glide must be considered, by the novice in particular, as a method of arriving in good position to put whilst on the move. Never utilize so much speed that you are unable to control the co-ordinated movements involved in delivering the shot correctly from a position of maximum advantage.

Preliminary Movements of the Glide

This is the beginning of the effort and it is essential for the athlete to relax momentarily and concentrate on the sequence of movements that are to follow. When the moment has come to start, the glide should begin by raising the left leg backwards along the line of the direction of put. At the same time the body should bend forward from the hips, which has the same effect of bringing the shot and shoulders outside the circumference of the circle. The athlete's body is now almost horizontal and parallel to the ground in a 'T' position over the right leg. He will be up on the ball of the right foot at this stage and the novice may well find this a position of precarious balance.

From this position the athlete should lower the body by allowing the knee to flex, at the same time bending and lowering the left leg which was out high behind him. The left thigh is now brought in towards the right leg (this part of the action should not be exgagerated) and then swung up and backwards towards the middle of the stopboard. A good instruction to the beginner at this point is to tell him to 'reach with the heel of the left foot'. At the same time the athlete should overbalance backwards, driving off the right leg and foot. The lifting of the left thigh has the effect of keeping the body down during the glide, so although he will arrive in the throwing stance with the trunk in a slightly higher position than that with which he started the glide, it will still be a comparatively low and power-ful position.

The Glide

The athlete is now moving across the circle rapidly and the right foot must be snapped quickly across the surface of the concrete as soon as it has completed its drive. The sole of the foot should barely break contact with the ground in this very rapid shift, the toes of the foot turning in and to the right at the same time as the whole leg and foot snap forward and under the bodyweight. The right foot must land with the toes directed not less than 45 degrees to the rear, otherwise the athlete will not be able to get his hip into the put effectively. The distance across the circle to where the foot lands will depend on a number of factors: the height of the athlete, his speed across the circle and the amount of lean-back he has in the throwing position. This in turn, will depend largely upon his general strength. However, as a rough guide it should land round about the centre line of the circle.

Since the shoulders and hips are facing directly to the rear during the glide, the left leg must move slightly across and to the left during the movement across the circle. If it goes straight back, it will land in line with the right foot or even to the right, which, in turn, will have the effect of blocking the hips during the put. The left foot should land approximately in line with the heel of the right foot and close to the stopboard. If it goes too far to the left, it is an equally bad fault so the placement of the left foot is a very important factor in shot putting.

The Delivery

The right foot lands before the left and a powerful rock-up begins with a vicious explosion off the right leg, the left leg staying relaxed, the foot coming naturally to the ground shortly after the right and in its correct position. The left knee should not be locked but remain slightly flexed in order to facilitate the movement of the body over the leg. When finally the body is over the left foot and the arm is beginning to strike, the left leg contributes its drive with a powerful straightening of the knee.

As the body lifts, the athlete should remain looking back at his marker for as long as he possibly can. When he can no longer sight his marker, the chin and eyes should be directed upwards, the right shoulder and elbow beginning to lift high. The rotation of the shoulders should come as late as possible; it is important first of all to concentrate on a lifting and a forward movement of the upper body.

As the shoulders begin to rotate to the front, the left side of the body must maintain its role of resisting the drive of the right side and at the same time the right shoulder and elbow come round in a high position. When the shoulders are almost square to the front, the right arm comes in with a powerful thrust. If all the previous movements have been timed correctly, and the shot is travelling fast when it leaves the hand, the final delivery will be completed with the wrist and finger flick.

The Reverse

The reverse should never be attempted until it is required. It will not be required until such time as the athlete is putting so well that he finds himself falling out of the circle at the end of his put. When the right leg has driven really well and effectively and the action has been timed correctly, the athlete will be well over the left foot as the arm strikes. Immediately after the shot has left the hand, he will find himself falling over the stop-board. In order to prevent himself fouling, the left foot is rapidly withdrawn and the right leg brought forward, the toes of the right foot striking the inside edge of the stopboard. At the same time the body weight is lowered in order to be more on balance by lowering the centre of gravity. However, the novice should remember that as a basic rule the left foot should not break contact with the ground until such time as the shot has left the hand. He will see world-class performers continually contravene this basic principle of all throwing events, but there are very good reasons for this, with which he need not concern himself at this stage.

Learning to put

1. You should commence be getting the feel of a standing put with a light shot. Drive with your right side and resist with your left side.

2. Now place the pole-vault stands about 6 ft in front of the circle with the bar at 9 ft. You should practise putting for height from a standing put position in the front of the circle. Use your right leg and drive up, get the right shoulder high and get the feeling of lifting upwards and forwards.

3. The glide should now be learnt by first of all doing a series of glide hops. Assume your starting position with the weight on the right foot and carry out a series of backward hops,

keeping the right foot very close to the surface of the ground. Your weight should remain on the back (right) foot throughout and the left leg assist with momentum and in keeping the trunk low and back by the left thigh being lifted in time with the thrust of the right leg. Once this has been mastered you should practise the glide as one movement in the circle without the shot. It will be found best to work along a line of direction marked on the concrete; you can then check your finishing position on each occasion.

4. Now practise the full glide and delivery from the circle. Don't forget to put the stopboard in position because practice should always be under the same conditions as you will have in competition.

5. As time goes on you should practise with an overweight shot. If you are using a 12 lb shot in competition then do standing puts with 18 lb, 16 lb and 14 lb shots in that order. Finish off with a full glide-and-put session with the 12 lb shot. The overweight shot must be weighted to suit your physical capabilities and it would be as well to consult an expert before deciding with what weights to practice.

6. Timing is the most important factor in shot putting. Therefore, you must practise the full glide and put, concentrating on the correct synchronization of leg, trunk and arm, each force taking over as the previous one finishes. Correct timing will come only by constant practise.

Winter Training

OCTOBER–MARCH

During this out-of-season period the beginner should carry out a lot of putting, working on the basic points of technique. This is one of the few events which need not be drastically curtailed owing to inclement weather conditions. In cold weather a bucket of hot water and some rags are a great asset. The shots should be placed in the bucket of water while the athlete is warming up in preparation for his session of putting. In this way they will be kept warm and can easily be cleaned before the next attempt on to frozen muddy ground. At this stage there is no point in worrying about the putting arm getting tired; the athlete may do anything from 50 to 100 or more puts at one session. However, each throw must be intelligently carried out; there is little point or use in throwing just for the sake of throwing. The athlete's concentration should be on one aspect of his technique on each delivery. Indoor throwing may be carried out with an indoor shot, or, if a net is available, with a metal shot into a throwing net fixed in a gymnasium.

Work for strength and speed must be done throughout the winter months, and indeed on throughout the season. The ambitious shot putter must continually be increasing the load of weight training, circuit training and perhaps isometric training that he is doing. By far the most important of these three is, of course, weight training. Some coaches would argue logically that circuit training is of little value to the shot putter and that he will get all he requires from weight training and sprinting. The shot putter is after all-round strength, so that a general schedule is most suitable for the novice. This should include 'presses', bench presses', 'squats', 'abdominal curls', the 'clean and jerk' and possibly the 'snatch'. These last two Olympic lifts are suggested for speed and agility and can be given to the big man who wants to get fast and agile. If the novice has no previous experience of weight training, then he must first of all have a groundwork of basic training. He will not be able to go straight on to advanced weight training such as the 'snatch or 'clean and jerk'. For further details of weight training for throwers turn to pages 160–3.

A typical schedule for this period might go something like this:

Monday

(a) Warm-up consisting of two laps' jogging, followed by a series of wind sprints. After this general mobilizing exercises should be carried out with particular attention paid to the arms, shoulders and back.
(b) Putting (20 min).
(c) Weight training.
(d) Warm-down (jogging).

Tuesday

(a) Warm-up (as before).
(b) Putting (until tired).
(c) Warm-down (jogging).

Wednesday

(a) Warm-up (as before).
(b) Weight training.
(c) Warm-down (jogging).

Thursday

Rest.

Friday

(a) Warm-up (as before).
(b) Weight training.
(c) Warm-down (jogging) 800m.

Saturday

(a) Warm-up (as before).
(b) Putting (until tired).
(c) Warm-down (jogging) 800 m.

Sunday

Rest.

On Monday the workout should occasionally be altered so that the 20 min of putting comes after the weight training.

APRIL–MAY

There should be no marked changes during this period. How-ever, the sessions will get longer and more intensive as the nights get longer and the better weather approaches. Sprinting and low hurdling will help at this stage.

Monday

(a) Warm-up (as before).
(b) Putting (until tired).
(c) Low hurdling (10 min).
(d) Warm-down (jogging 800 m).

Tuesday

(a) Warm-up (as before).
(b) Weight training .
(c) Warm-down (jogging 800 m).

Wednesday

(a) Warm-up (as before).
(b) Putting (30 min).
(c) Low hurdling (10 min)
(d) Warm-down (jogging 800 m).

Thursday

(a) Warm-up (as before).
(b) Weight training.

(c) Sprinting (short dashes of 60 m) 10 min.
(d) Warm-down (jogging 800 m).

Friday
Rest.

Saturday
Competition.

Sunday

(a) Warm-up (as before).
(b) Weight training.
(c) Warm-down (jogging 800 m).

JUNE–AUGUST

The training sessions lighten as the competitive season reaches its height. Weight training should be continued on two days per week and another day might well be spent doing isometric work as a variation.

Monday

(a) Warm-up (as before).
(b) Putting (30 min working on faults which may have occurred in Saturday's competition).
(c) Weight training.
(d) Warm-down (jogging 800 m).

Tuesday

(a) Warm-up (as before).
(b) Sprinting (short dashes of 60 in with the sprinters).
(c) Warm-down (800 m jogging).

Wednesday

(a) Warm-up (as before).
(b) Putting (30 min for form).
(c) Weight training.
(d) Warm-down (800 m jogging).

Thursday

(a) Warm-up (as before).
(b) Sprint starts with the sprinters (15 min).
(c) Low hurdling (15 min).
(d) Warm-down (jogging 800 m).

Friday

Rest.

Saturday

Competition.

Sunday

(a) Warm-up (as before).
(b) Isometric work.
(c) Light sprinting.
(d) Warm-down (jogging 800 m).

(i)   (ii)   (iii)

(iv)   (v)   (vi)

(i) The athlete is in a standing position facing to the rear of the circle The toes of the right foot are pointing directly to the rear and the head and eyes are directly at a marker situated some 10 ft- 15 ft directly behind the circle. The toes of the left foot are gently tapping the ground some 10–15 in. towards the front of the circle. The weight is entirely on the right foot and the shot held in the manner described at the beginning of the chapter. The left arm is raised above the head, the palm of the hand facing towards the rear.

(ii) The bodyweight has been lowered and the left leg which was out behind the athlete has been bent and lowered slightly, the left thigh being brought in towards the right. The right elbow is in line with the right knee and the left arm in a relaxed position of balance. The movement across the circle now commences.

(iii) Here he has overbalanced backwards and is driving off the right leg and foot. The lifting of the left leg is keeping the body low during the glide. The shoulders must be kept back at this stage, it is a great temptation to the novice to 'open out' prematurely and arrive in a putting position with the shoulders already partially turned to the front. Note the position of the left arm which assists in keeping the shoulders back.

(iv) The right foot has been snapped quickly under the body-weight, the foot landing approximately on the centre line of the circle. The position is slightly higher than that shown at the commencement of the shift. However, this is to be expected; the shot will gradually rise from the rear to the front of the circle. Though the novice must remember to keep low as one of the most common faults with the beginner is to be too upright in the putting stance.

(v) The right leg is completing its drive and the shoulders are turning to the front right elbow and shoulder coming through high. The left leg is bent at the knee with the whole of the left side braced. The left arm has been bent and brought down and back from this position the right arm is beginning to strike.

(vi) The athlete is now well over the left foot which is close up to the stepboard. The right arm is completing its thrust and the left leg has straightened to complete its drive. Note that there has been no break at the hips; this is a very common fault with the beginner and boys who are not strong enough to handle the implement. Once the shot has left the hand the reverse may commence.

10. The Javelin

The good javelin thrower is to be found amongst the boys who can throw cricket balls or stones a long way. A boy who has thrown hard when he was young (between the ages of six and twelve) will have developed his arm and shoulder correctly for throwing the javelin. The shoulder must be supple as well as strong, hence the coach often finds that the boy who swims well has the necessary mobility in the shoulder to produce sufficient range of movement to be able to be pull along the length of the javelin and apply his force over a great distance.

This is an exacting event: the skills of lining the javelin up correctly, running with the javelin and directing the force through the point must be learnt first. Wild, undisciplined throwing for distance will produce very little improvement. The coach must stand behind the young thrower for the first month of the learning period, seeing that he produces a technically correct throw below maximum effort. In this way he will learn to throw on the run with the javelin held in the correct position and be able to apply his force along the direction of flight.

The Grip

The javelin must be held at the binding with at least one finger behind the binding and the shaft itself lying along the groove of the palm of the hand. The palm of the hand is a platform on which the binding of the javelin should rest right up to the moment of release. It is better to grip too tightly behind the binding than to have a hold at this point which is too slack. Generally speaking, it is best to place the middle finger behind the binding, the first finger curling comfortably around the shaft behind. The remaining digits should be folded firmly around the binding to hold the javelin in its place against the pad of the thumb and the outside pad below the little finger. Remember the grip is all-important – the javelin should be thrown off the palm of the hand and the shaft never allowed to come off the palm before release, thereby throwing with the fingers alone. This is one of the most common faults of the beginner, causing the point to fly too high, and a very poor delivery is the result.

Two other grips are worth mentioning. Firstly, the first and middle fingers are placed behind the binding, the shaft resting in the fork made by the two fingers. One advantage of this grip is that the javelin lies more easily in the palm of the hand and more in line with the forearm. Most first-class throwers use this grip with advantage; if the young thrower should try it and dislike it immediately, it is sound advice to persevere with it for a while. Anything new feels strange to begin with, but with a little practice the thrower may become accustomed to it and ultimately find it suits him better. Secondly, some throwers prefer to place the first finger behind the binding. The beginner very often finds this hold easier to manage but it is not necessarily the best method for him to adopt.

The Throwing Position

The basic throwing position is comparatively simple. The thrower should stand with feet astride, facing forwards, with the weight over the rear foot. The shoulders and upper body should now be turned to the side with the arm extended directly behind and the hand held high in line with the shoulders. The non-throwing arm should be folded across but not against the chest and underneath the point of the javelin. The feet and hips must not be turned to the side either during the approach or in the throwing position. If they are turned to the side, the thrower will find it impossible to throw on the run.

Note the following points:

1. The shaft of the javelin should be in line with your eyes.

2. Your head and eyes should be directed at the point.

3. Your front shoulder should be high and arm folded round underneath the point.

4. Both shoulders and the hand of your throwing arm should be in line.

5. Your weight should be on the ball of your rear foot, knee bent, toes pointed forward.

6. Your front leg should be nearly straight, heel in contact with the ground.

7. Now lean well back, making certain that the tail of the javelin is clear of the ground.

8. Your hips and legs are now virtually in a running position with the upper body turned to the right.

Learning to Throw

For the right-handed thrower the javelin should be held over the head, the right wrist gripped firmly in the left hand, knuckles facing back. He should now step in with the left foot, taking both arms as far behind as possible. The thrower is now in a position facing forwards but leaning back, arms extended behind and left foot advanced. From this position he should learn to throw from over the head, using the back correctly. Most novices never get the elbow up and as a result throw round the shoulder. The left hand holding the right hand in position gives him the feeling of throwing correctly from the beginning.

The athlete should now learn to throw on the run off three strides. For a right-handed thrower this means a left-right-left rhythm with the feet. Stand with the feet together, with the javelin held back and high in the position previously described .On the second stride the right foot crosses in front of the left leg. This has been referred to in the past as the cross-step and great emphasis has been placed on this movement. In actual fact, it is merely a running stride with the upper body turned to the right. During this stride you gather for the throw, leaning back a bit more and relaxing ready for the throw. When throwing with a full run, the javelin will have been taken back two strides before the cross-step and all the major adjustments to body position made already.

The right foot should come to the ground, heel and outside of the foot first, at the completion of the cross-step. Don't turn the toes to the right under any circumstances.

The run should now be taken back to five strides and this now becomes the basic skill or fundamental practice of javelin throwing, starting in the same manner with the feet together, facing forwards, javelin held back and high, hand in line with the shoulder. The thrower should now start his run with the left foot to a five-count rhythm, leaning back and relaxing on the fourth count.

The Throw

Note the following instructions;

1. Line the implement up correctly. To do this, watch the point and keep the shaft in line with the eyes.

2. Start the throw early as you land on the right foot. The throw is a long pull and begins by running on your right

foot against the resistance of your left foot. Do not use the arm yet; keep it back, completely relaxed.

3. As the heel of your left foot comes down to the ground well out in advance of your body, your right shoulder should begin to lift and as the ball of the foot comes down an instant later you should think of pulling forward and upward with the shoulder.

4. The right elbow now rotates out and up as the upper arm comes in, the throw finishes with a final flail-like action of the lower arm.

5. Watch the point of the javelin and throw through the point.

6. Keep the javelin in the whole of your hand throughout the throw and release it off the platform of the palm of your hand.

7. Remember this is a throw on the run, so keep moving.

8. Allow a javelin's length from the position of your left foot in the throwing stance to the line for the reverse. If you have thrown on the run, you will require this distance in order to stay behind the arc.

Throwing with a full Run

The athlete should now start to handle an overhead carry. It should be carried over the head, point up, lying along the direction of throw. The take-back should start some distance before the cross-step and the javelin be withdrawn along the line of throw. In this way the thrower has only one action to learn: backwards and then forwards along the same line of direction. The take-back and correct line-up are two of the major factors in good javelin throwing. Until the young thrower has mastered this skill, he will never throw well or consistently.

It is best to take the javelin back steadily and not to hurry this movement; it must be practised assiduously until perfected.

The javelin must be in position for the throw a *least* two strides before the cross-step. This allows time for the novice to line it up correctly.

Training

Strength mobility and speed must be worked for during the winter months. Mobility exercises are essential if the thrower is to be supple enough to get into a good throwing position with the arm extended full to the rear, also to obtain a wide throwing base and from this position to use the body effectively in the delivery.

Very few throwers are anything like strong enough and, therefore, weight training and isometric work can be done with great advantage on at least three days per week. Every warm-up should include a series of suppling and strengthening exercises of gradually increasing intensity and range of movement.

At least two days should be devoted to mastering the skill of throwing the javelin. This includes careful adjustment of line-up and carry, which are perhaps the most important factors for the novice to master in the early stages of his career. Throwing with a 4 lb or 6 lb weight is a recommended activity from a standing position and from one stride.

A typical week's work might go something like this:

Monday

(a) Warm-up: Consisting of two laps' jogging, followed by a series of strides down the straights covering about 80 m. After this do mobilizing exercises with particular emphasis on the arms, shoulders and back.

(b) Throwing: This may be done with a light weight to start with and then continue with throwing off a short run with the javelin. The athlete should concentrate on line-up and correct carriage and take-back of the implement. No attempt should be made to throw for distance off a full run at this stage.

(c) Warm-down: Consisting of light exercises and jogging two laps.

Tuesday

(a) Warm-up (as before).
(b) Some short interval running with bursts of speed over about 60 m.
(c) Weight training.

Wednesday

(a) Warm-up (as before).
(b) Light throwing from a short run (30 min).
(c) Warm-down (as before).

Thursday

(a) Warm-up (as before).
(b) Short interval running as suggested on Tuesday.
(c) Heavy weight-training session (40 min).

Friday

(a) Warm-up (as before).
(b) Throwing light weights (4 lb and 6 lb shot), concentrating on body pull.
(c) Warm-down (as before).

Saturday

(a) Warm-up.
(b) Weight training (30 min).

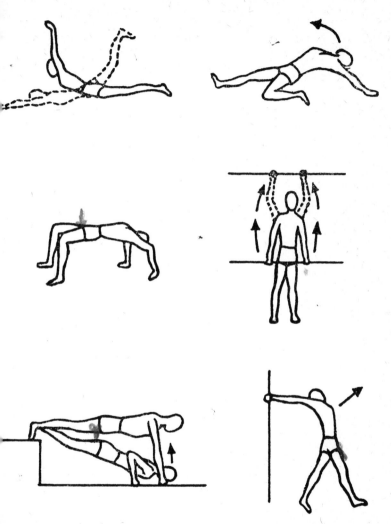

Shows a typical set of limbering-up excercises for javelin throwers.

(c) When possible, throwing can be done after the weight-training session. Concentrate on precise handling of the implement when tired.

(d) Warm-down (as before).

Sunday

Rest.

The same general plan of training can be continued except that the throwing sessions can be longer and more intensive. Weight training must also be continued but the days on which the sessions are carried out should be ajusted as competition begins towards the end of this period.

Monday

(a) Warm-up (as before).
(b) Light throwing, concentrate on line-up and throwing on the move.
(c) Weight training.
(d) Warm-down (as before).

Tuesday

(a) Warm-up (as before).
(b) Interval running with bursts of speed over 60 m.
(c) Throwing with a light weight.
(d) Warm-down (as before).

Wednesday

(a) Warm-up (as before).
(b) Hard throwing session.

(c) Weight training.
(d) Warm-down (as before).

Thursday

(a) Warm-up (as before).
(b) Light throwing for form.
(c) Warm-down (as before).

Friday

Rest.

Saturday

Competition.

Sunday

(a) Warm-up (as before).
(b) Sprint starting over 40 m.
(c) Throwing with a light weight.
(d) Warm-down (as before).

JUNE–AUGUST

The training sessions lighten as the competitive season reaches its height.

Monday

(a) Warm-up (as before).
(b) Light throwing for form.
(c) Weight training.
(d) Warm-down (as before).

Tuesday

(a) Warm-up (as before).

K

(i)   (ii)

(iii)   (iv)   (v)

(vi)   (vii)   (viii)

(i) Shows the thrower completing the stride before the cross-step. The left foot is coming to the ground and the right leg is beginning to come through into the cross-step. Note that the right hand and javelin are in line with both shoulders and the head and eyes are directed forwards.

(ii) The thrower is now in the middle of the cross-step. The feet, legs and hips are in a running position while the shoulders have turned to the right. The right hand is held in line with both shoulders and the left arm is wrapped across the chest underneath the javelin. The head and eyes are directed forwards at the point of the implement.

(iii) The right foot has now contacted the ground heel and outside of the foot first. The toes of the right foot are pointing forwards and to the right and the lower part of the body is still maintaining its running position with the hips directed forwards. The shoulders are turned to the right and the body leans well back. The right hand is still held high and the thrower's eyes are directed at the point of the javelin.

(iv) The body-pull is now taking place. Note that the right arm is still completely extended to the rear and the left foot is going out and forwards to form a wide throwing base. From this point onwards the thrower must attempt to keep the left shoulder going forwards for as long as possible. If the shoulders come round to the front too soon, the arm will come in to throw prematurely.

(v) The left foot is now in contact with the ground. The whole body is moving forwards and the rotation of the shoulders has begun but the arm is left behind until the last possible moment.

(vi) The right shoulders, upper arm and elbow are moving very rapidly forwards and upwards. The left leg is bent at the knee; this facilitates the hinging action of the body over the left side.

(vii) The throw is now complete; the lower arm has completed its flail-like action and the bodyweight comes up and over the left leg which has now straightened.

(viii) The bodyweight continues to come up and over the left leg and the right leg comes forward to provide a check to save fouling the line.

(b) Throwing session (30 min).
(c) Warm-up (as before).

Wednesday

(a) Warm-up (as before).
(b) Weight training (light session).
(c) Light throwing for form if necessary.
(d) Warm-down (as before).

Thursday

(a) Warm-up (as before).

(b) 60 m dashes or low hurdling.
(c) Warm-down (as before).

Friday
Rest.

Saturday
Competition.

11. The Discus

The modern discus thrower starts at the back of the circle facing the rear and turns through 450 degrees as opposed to the old method of facing sideways and turning through a simple 360 degrees. The extra quarter-turn gives the thrower a greater distance over which he can accelerate the discus. The subsequent turn which he performs is nowadays referred to as a 'Running Rotation' as opposed to the terms 'Pivot Rotation' and 'Jump Rotation', which have been used in the past to describe two different methods of throwing.

The Grip (right-handed thrower)

The discus should rest against the flat of the hand with the fingers spread comfortably, the pads of the first joints resting over the metal rim. It is important to remember that the implement should not be gripped but rather be allowed to rest in between the tips of the fingers and the first joints. The thumb should lie flat along the plate and will act as a stabilizer on delivery.

Preliminary Swings

The thrower should position himself at the rear of the circle with his back to the general line of direction. In training, a line should be drawn across the circle from back to front along the line of direction of the throw. This will act as a guide to the thrower in practice. He should now straddle this line with the feet placed either side of it about shoulder width apart, with the toes touching the inner edge of the circle.

The athlete should now hold the discus as previously described and do no more than two or three preliminary swings. The discus should be flat and facing downwards and the arm swung at shoulder height so that the arm and discus go well behind the right shoulder: meantime the left arm folds comfortably across the chest.

As the discus is swung forward it should again be kept flat and in line with the shoulders. At the end of its forward swing it can be received in the left hand to prevent it falling. On the back-swing some throwers like to supinate (turn up) the hand in order to prevent it falling. However, this should not be necessary really; it is a matter of confidence gained from experience.

The trunk must be kept erect during the swings and the thrower's weight should move easily from one foot to the other. As the disus swings to the right behind the shoulder, the thrower's weight will be distributed over the right leg and the left leg will flex at the knee and the heel will rise; the right leg will remain straight. On the forward swing the left leg will straighten and the bodyweight be transferred over it while the right leg will flex and the heel rise.

The purpose of swinging the discus in this way is to prepare the thrower mentally and physically for the throw. It allows him time to concentrate on what is to follow and also to get a secure hold of the discus. The feeling of the fingers on the rim of the implement must be just right before deciding to commence the turn and he must get the sensation of the correct rhythm and be relaxed.

The Turn

It is important to remember that in the turn the thrower is not only rotating but also moving across the circle along the line of direction of the throw and both these factors must take second place to a good throwing position. An effective throwing position is one of 'muscular unwind'—the hips displaced from the feet, shoulders from the hips, arm and discus from the shoulders. From such a position the thrower may explode powerfully into the throw, each part of the body adding its force as the previous force finishes. In this way the athlete obtains a well-timed delivery using the powerful muscles of the body first and finishing the throw with the light but fast arm which can further accelerate a discus already moving at great speed.

As the discus moves back on its last preliminary swing the thrower should turn the left foot, knee and hip in the direction of throw, the shoulders being kept back, the left arm wrapped across the chest to assist, The bodyweight should now move over the left foot, the right foot remaining in contact with the ground for as long as possible. The athlete is now in a position of torque, the hips ahead of the shoulders, the trunk erect, left shoulder high and legs splayed in a bandy position.

The thrower now overbalances, allowing the upper part of the body to get ahead of the left foot. The left leg now drives and the right thighs lifts, staying compact and close to the left. As the left foot leaves the ground, both feet are out of contact with the surface of the circle for a fraction of a second. This drive should carry the thrower halfway across the circle, the right foot landing approximately on the centre line with the leg well bent and the shoulders and bodyweight back. Meantime, the left leg should be moving rapidly towards the front of the circle in as straight a line as possible. The quicker the left foot is down in position to provide a resistance to the throwing side the better. The athlete should now be in a wound-up position about a vertical axis, the right toes pointing at about 45 degrees to the rear, right knee bent and bodyweight disposed over the leg. The right arm and discus should be trailing well behind the shoulder, the discus held in the hand, palm down, knuckles up and approximately in line with the shoulder.

The Throw

The throw begins with a forward and upward drive from the right foot. The foot must turn in very rapidly in order to drive the hips round ahead of the shoulder, arm and discus. The shoulder should now come in slightly after the hip and the arm strikes from the low point, the thrower reaching out as far as posible to give as much distance from the axis of rotation as he can. At the same time it is vitally important to keep the whole body going forward for as long as posisble.

The left leg, which although acting as a firm brace has remained slightly bent, should now straighten as the arm strikes. This important left leg drive gives the discus lift on delivery. The discus will leave the hand in line with the right shoulder and should be squeezed out of the fingers, each digit applying its force in turn, and spinning off the first finger last. This rotational effect is vitally important because the spin gives the discus stability in flight.

The Reverse

The reverse will be required only at the end of a good throw where the thrower has driven his bodyweight well over the left foot on delivery. It is best not to teach the reverse until such time as the athlete is throwing well enough to require it.

After the discus has left the hand, the thrower will have to reverse the feet rapidly and lower the bodyweight to maintain balance. The right leg must be brought forward quickly and planted firmly close to the rim of the circle, the left leg meantime swings back. The body is bent at the hips and the right knee flexes to drop the centre of gravity into a stable position.

Some throwers, as a result of a rather narrow throwing base and a very powerful drive from the legs, may start the reverse very slightly before the discus has left the hand. This is not recommended for the novice who will tend to jump into the throw, which is an extremely bad fault.

Learning to throw

1. Get the feeling of the preliminary swings by practising easy swings using the correct hold as described previously. At this stage make your swing low in order to get used to the hold and gain confidence.

2. Practise preliminary swings at shoulder height in the correct manner. Make these swings as easy and relaxed as possible. Try to avoid having to supinate the hand on the back-swing; if you have to, remember to turn it down again as you begin the forward swing.

3. Now hold the discus correctly and, stooping down, bowl the discus along the ground in order to get the feeling of a correct release.

4. Go to the circle and stand side-on to the line of direction of throw and practise standing throws after two or three easy preliminary swings. Gradually increase the width of your throwing base by placing your feet further apart, at the same time, as you gain confidence, twist the shoulders further to the rear, before commencing each delivery.

5. Now you should practice the turn along a line of direction drawn across the circle. First of all do this without the discus, landing looking back at an object placed on the ground about 10 yd out to your right and to the rear.

(i)   (ii)   (iii)

(iv)   (v)   (vi)

(i) Shows the athlete towards the completion of the last preliminary swing. Note that the left arm is wrapped across the
chest in order to assist in holding the shoulders back as he goes
into the turn. The trunk is erect and the athlete is in a semi-
sitting position with the bodyweight over the right leg.

(ii) The left foot, knee and hip have moved into the turn and the
bodyweight shifted over on to the left leg. The legs are in the
bandy position, the athlete sitting with the trunk erect as he
begins the drive across the circle. The discus trails behind the
right shoulder and the left arm is kept back and across the chest.
The left shoulder is kept high and is held back and behind the
left hip which leads into the turn.

(iii) The left leg is completing its drive and the right thigh has
been picked up high. The lower parts of the body (legs and hips)
are moving fast to get ahead of the shoulders. Note that the
discus is trailing well behind the right shoulder.

(iv) The right knee has been kept flexed and the thrower has
landed on a bent right leg with the upper body well back over
the leg and towards the back of the circle. The right foot should

be well turned in to assist the torque. The left leg is moving rapidly towards the front of the circle.

(v) The athlete is now in the throwing position with the left foot down on the ground. The throw is beginning with the right knee turning in and the leg driving. Note that the hips are displaced from the feet, shoulders from the hips and the right arm and discus trailing behind the shoulders.

(vi) The vigorous action of the right leg has driven the hips round to the front. The shoulders have come round shortly after the hip and the arm, wrist and fingers are about to dispatch the discus. Note the flat discus, it is only slightly inclined upwards on delivery. The left leg has just contributed its important drive as the arm strikes.

6. Finally, tack the turn on to your standing throw. First of all concentrate on landing in a good throwing position. Do not attempt to obtain too much speed in the beginning.

Winter Training

OCTOBER–MARCH

During this period the beginner should carry out as much throwing for technique as he possibly can. It is during the winter months that the young thrower should lay the foundations of a sound technique which can be polished and improved in the spring and early summer. Owing to inclement weather and lack of proper indoor facilities, young throwers in this country are often badly handicapped through the inability to practise the event during severe weather conditions. In this case, a throwing net placed in a gymnasium can be an invaluable aid. The athlete can now practise the complete throw and release into the net. When throwing is done outside in bad weather, it is essential to have a selection of dry cloths available in order to keep the discus dry for throwing. Once the rim of the discus gets wet it becomes impossible to handle.

Weight training for strength must be done throughout the winter and should be continued in a slightly more limited manner throughout the competitive season. Isometric work can also be included, especially as a substitute for some weight-training sessions during the summer months. Circuit training can also be done but this is of limited value to the thrower who is basically after pure strength. However, as a general conditioner for the young athlete it can be very useful. Some sprinting should be done for speed and general fitness; it is often difficult to convince throwers that this is necessary but speed is the basis of all throwing events. The technique of throwing events is designed to obtain as much speed as possible on delivery of the missile. Hence throwers need not only to be strong but also fast and agile.

A typical schedule for this period might go something like this:

Monday

(a) Warm-up consisting of two laps' jogging followed by a series of wind sprints. After this, general mobilizing exercises should be carried out with particular emphasis on the arms, shoulders and back.
(b) Throwing into a net indoors (20 min).
(c) Weight training.
(d) Warm-down (jogging).

Tuesday

(a) Warm-up (as before).
(b) Throwing, concentrating on points of technique (40 min). This session should be done out of doors. weather permitting.
(c) Warm-down (jogging).

Wednesday

(a) Warm-up (as before).
(b) Weight training.
(c) Warm-down (jogging).

Thursday
Rest.

Friday

(a) Warm-up (as before).
(b) Short dashes over 60 m (15 min).
(c) Weight training.
(d) Warm-down (jogging 800 m).

Saturday

(a) Warm-up (as before).
(b) Hard throwing until tired.
(c) Warm-down (jogging 800 m).

Sunday
Rest.

On Monday the workout should occasionally be altered so that the throwing comes after the weight training. When it is impossible to throw outside owing to inclement weather, try and substitute with indoor throwing into a net.

APRIL–MAY

There should be no major alterations to the schedule during this period. However, the intensity of the training will increase as the lighter evenings and better weather begin to appear. Technique can be polished up in warm dry weather outside and low hurdling may be added to sprinting for speed and agility. The weight training must be continued and isometric work added if required.

Monday

(a) Warm-up (as before).
(b) Throwing for form, concentrating on any faults that might have occured in Saturday's competition.
(c) 8 × 60 m dashes with 3 min recovery between.
(d) Warm-down (jogging 800 m).

Tuesday

(a) Warm-up (as before).
(b) Weight training.
(c) Warm-down (jogging 800 m).

Wednesday

(a) Warm-up (as before).
(b) Throwing (30 min).
(c) Low hurdling (10 min).
(d) Warm-down (jogging 800 m).

Thursday

(a) Warm-up (as before).
(b) Weight training.
(c) Sprint starts over 40 m.
(d) Warm-down (jogging 800 m).

Friday

Rest.

Saturday

Competition.

Sunday

(a) Warm-up (as before).
(b) Weight training.
(c) Warm-down (jogging 800 m).

The work should lighten as the competitive season reaches its height. Weight training should be continued on two days per week and another session might also be devoted to isometric work.

Monday

(a) Warm-up (as before).
(b) Throwing (working on faults that might have occurred during Saturday's competition).
(c) Weight training.
(d) Warm-down (jogging 800 m).

Tuesday

(a) Warm-up (as before).
(b) Low hurdling (10 min).
(c) 6×60 m dashes with 3 min recovery.
(d) Warm-down (jogging 800 m).

Wednesday

(a) Warm-up (as before).
(b) Throwing (30 min).
(c) Weight training.
(d) Warm-down (jogging 800 m).

Thursday

(a) Warm-up (as before).
(b) Sprint starts with the sprinters over 40 m.

(c) Low hurdling (10 min).
(d) Warm-down (jogging 800 m).

Friday
Rest.

Saturday
Competition.

Sunday

(a) Warm-up (as before).
(a) Isometric work.
(c) Light sprinting.
(d) Warm-down (jogging 800 m).

Weight Training for Throwers

Technique and strength go hand in hand, particularly in the throwing events where a heavy implement is being handled. Young throwers are very often not strong enough to handle the shot, discus or javelin properly. In this case it is little use the coach attempting to improve their technique until such time as they have developed their physique by forms of progressive resistance work, such as weight training and isometric training.

Weight training for throwing and, indeed, for all events should be general, not just applied to those muscle groups which directly affect the performance of the event. It is total body strength that counts; one group of muscles is dependent on another; even the distance runner requires well-developed arms as well as his naturally strong legs. Certainly there have been exceptions to this rule but they have succeeded in spite of their deficiencies in strength, certainly not because of them.

Broadly speaking, there are two ways of tackling weight training:

1. Large number of repetitions with light weights.
2. Few repetitions with a heavy load for strength.

In the first method the young thrower might be doing three sets of ten repetitions while he learns the skills involved in weight training and builds up his physique in preparation for a more advanced schedule to follow.

In the second method the athlete might be doing three sets of five repetitions with a much heavier poundage in order to produce all-round strength as quickly as possible. There are three things to remember about the more advanced schedule to which the young thrower should progress as quickly as possible:

1. The weights being handled must be heavy and, therefore, repetitions few.
2. The repetitions must be of the maximum number that the athlete is capable of at the time.
3. As the strength of the athlete improves, so must the weight being handled increase.

There are many other methods of tackling weight training, including working to a decreasing number of repetitions and increasing poundage with each lift, for example:

Barbell Squats

5 repetitions at 120 lb
4 repetitions at 130 lb
3 repetitions at 140 lb
2 repetitions at 150 lb
1 repetition at 160 lb

In this case the poundage must be so arranged that the last repetition is at maximum effort and this is the one that does most good. However, the young thrower is well advised to make his schedules as simple and concentrated as possible. Here is a utility schedule which has been carried out by a young shot putter throwing approximately 50 ft with the 16 lb weight. This workout will take approximately 1½ hours to complete and the athlete might well find it benefical to drink a pint of milk during this period.

Squats

4 repetitions at 392 lb
4 repetitions at 402 lb
4 repetitions at 412 lb
4 repetitions at 422 lb

Behind Neck Press

4 repetitions at 200 lb
4 repetitions at 205 lb
4 repetitions at 210 lb
4 repetitions at 215 lb

Clean and Jerk

1 repetition at 250 lb
1 repetition at 260 lb
1 repetition at 270 lb

Bench Press

5 repetitions at 290 lb
5 repetitions at 300 lb
5 repetitions at 310 lb
5 repetitions at 320 lb

Snatch

1 repetition at 160 lb
1 repetition at 170 lb
1 repetition at 180 lb
1 repetition at 190 lb
1 repetition at 200 lb

It must be remembered that the poundages in this schedule are suited to one individual and it would be quite wrong for another thrower to take on this schedule exactly as it stands. This particular athlete had, at this time only just commenced the clean and jerk and snatch. Hence it may be seen that the weight is not high in either lift in relation to his actual strength.

Once the young thrower has carried out a novice schedule for a while, he might carry out a schedule including the following exercises doing three sets of five repetitions in the beginning:

1. High pull-ups.
2. Press.
3. Clean and jerk.
4. Squats or straddle lift.
5. Abdominal.
6. Specialist exercise directly applying to his event.

12. Diet and Isometric Training

Diet

Although there is as much team spirit among athletes competing in school, club or international competition as there is in any other sport, basically it is the individual and his personal performance that counts. This tends to lead to individualism among athletes and, as a result, a small percentage become introspective and fussy about their personal habits and way of life. Unimportant things sometimes become very important and molehills tend to loom up as mountains on the horizon. Sometimes after listening to an athlete expounding his ideas and troubles, his coach has to tap him on the head and say: 'If you can get out of there, you'll find it's not so bad out here.' This is fortunately the exception and not the rule. Nevertheless many a brilliant athlete has failed to get the best out of himself because of worry about unimportant details and the continual turning inwards of his thoughts.

One of the most common manifestations of this is the athlete with a restless and unnatural quest for the ideal diet, the wonder vitamin pill that will transform him into a champion next season. As a young athlete, be on your guard because you may well be selected by one of these young men as the audience he requires in order to convince himself that at long last he has found the answer. He will deliver a dissertation on diet second to none; you will be baffled by long words and vitamins you never realized existed. Our dietitian may not even realize it but he is exploiting to the full one of the most successful ploys of 'Gamesmanship' ever devised. You have never had the advantage of these preparations, you never realized the importance of eating exactly the right food at exactly the right time, you feel inferior and quite inadequate. This is not one of the normal dressing-room ploys easily detected and just as easily deflected but a subtle slow working poison that strikes at the very centre of your being. Your vital organs, muscle tissue and even bones become affected, you feel dizzy and weak from lack of proper nourishment. You don't think you're going to run very well that afternoon!

Here are a few simple rules which will be a useful guide on what and when to eat and how best to supplement your diet:

1. It is better to eat a little and often rather than to have a few heavy meals during the day. This does not mean one should eat more but it is better to have four or five small meals rather than two or three large ones. Long intervals between meals are bad. The last meal before competition should be taken 3 to 4 hours before the start.

2. For long-distance events stop heavy work 48 hours before competition. This allows the body's store of carbohydrate to build up. Most long-distance runs are made using up the carbohydrate in the body to provide energy. Shift to fairly high carbohydrate foods before racing.

3. A moderate excess of high-quality protein, i.e. steak, meat in general, fish, eggs, cheese and milk will not increase efficiency in terms of performance but will ensure that any growth requirements are met satisfactorily. Athletes undergoing a tough regimen in training such as weight training and hard physical exercise are well advised to increase their protein intake.

4. A lot of glucose taken during competition is not good as it

draws moisture for its digestion and therefore accelerates the dehydration of the body. Athletes competing in hot climates should take particular note not to overdo their glucose intake.

5. Coffee and tea have a depressant effect 2 to 3 hours later. Therefore, they might affect performance if taken at the last meal before competition.

6. A diet deficient in vitamin A does not produce any marked decrease in physical efficiency. Vitamin B deficiency results in fatigue, loss of ambition and efficiency. Supplementation of vitamin will decrease the fatiguability of the central nervous system and improve reaction time in both trained and untrained athletes. Brewer's yeast will remedy any deficiency of vitamin B. Vitamin C may increase resistance to colds and minor infections but has little, if any, physical effect. There is a case for supplementation though in winter when green vegetables are not readily available. There is no clear demonstration of the benefical effects of vitamin E supplementation.

Isometric Training

The word isometric means evenness of length and involves a series of maximum contractions against an immovable object in various positions. This type of work can increase strength at a remarkable rate if done regularly. The athlete might well find it beneficial as a means of maintaining strength quickly and easily during the summer months.

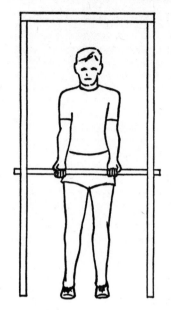

A simple piece of apparatus for carrying out a suitable isometric schedule for athletes. The uprights are slotted to take the adjustable horizontal bar, i.e. cross section shown in the diagram.

The fixed horizontal bar at the top not only fixes the uprights but also acts as a bar for chins and normal horizontal bar work. This can be of great use to pole vaulters and throwers in particular.

Schedule

Presses

Force applied at:
1. The level of the chin.
2. The level of the forehead.
3. Just below complete extension of the arms.

Pulls

Force applied at:
1. Level of the knees.
2. Level of the waist.
3. Just below the armpits.

Squats

Force applied at:
1. Full squat position (thighs parallel to the ground).
2. Squat with thighs just above the parallel position.
3. Quarter squat position.

Employ all exercises once per day applying your force for 8 sec at maximum. Take 1 min rest between exercises and change the position of the bar during this break.